Scenic Stays

The RV Camper's Journey Through National Parks

Anna Brown

Table of Contents

INTRODUCTION

"Scenic Stays: The RV Camper's Journey Through National Parks" takes readers on an exciting journey through some of the most breathtaking scenery in the United States. We warmly request you to join us on this thrilling adventure, which is the ultimate road trip experience: a leisurely drive in the luxury of your own RV through the nation's most beloved National Parks.

As we embark on this incredible journey, you'll come to appreciate the remarkable beauty and breathtaking wonder of our nation's most famous natural wonders. From the majestic peaks of the Rocky Mountains to the rugged wilderness of Alaska's Wrangell-St. Elias National Park, every chapter of this book is a gateway to new horizons, a doorway to unforgettable memories.

This book is a thorough companion for both RV enthusiasts and nature lovers, serving as more than just a travel guide. Whether you're an experienced camper or a first-time traveler, we offer priceless planning insights, vital RV camping advice, and thorough descriptions of every National Park, complete with must-see sights, RV campgrounds, and insider tips to maximize your trip.

Come along with us as we embark on a journey to rediscover nature, relish stunning sunsets, and pay attention to the whispers of the wild. "Scenic Stays" provides the flexibility to travel, the excitement of experiencing new things, and the spirit of discovery, making it your pass to America's natural wonders. So, fuel up your RV, pack your sense of wonder, and let's hit the road together on an unforgettable odyssey through the National Parks of the United States.

CHAPTER I

Planning Your National Park Adventure

Choosing the right RV and equipment

When starting your journey through the National Parks, an essential first step is selecting the appropriate RV and gear. Your RV camping experience's comfort, convenience, and overall enjoyment may all be significantly impacted by this choice. As a result, it's critical to weigh your options and make wise decisions thoroughly.

You must first choose the kind of RV that best fits your requirements and tastes. There are various options to select from, such as camper vans, fifth wheels, travel trailers, and motorhomes. Motorhomes are perfect for long-distance travelers who desire all the comforts of home while traveling. They come in three different classes (Class A, B, and C) and provide the convenience of a self-contained living space. Contrarily, fifth wheels and travel trailers allow you to tow your RV with a different car, making it simple to disengage and explore in your car or truck after you've set up camp. For travelers who want a more simplified travel experience, couples or lone travelers may choose the small, adaptable camper van.

Another crucial aspect to consider is your RV's size. In the context of National Parks, smaller RVs offer the advantage of easy maneuverability and suitability for navigating curves and narrow roads. They also tend to be more fuel-efficient, making them a cost-effective choice. However, larger RVs, despite their reduced maneuverability and fuel efficiency, provide higher comfort with their spacious living areas and amenities. Striking a balance between comfort and size that aligns with your travel goals is key.

After deciding on the style and dimensions of your RV, you also need to consider its amenities and features. Various amenities are available in many contemporary RVs, such as entertainment systems, sleeping areas, kitchens, and bathrooms. Examine your unique requirements and tastes to ensure your chosen RV has the desired amenities. For example, having a well-stocked kitchen with a stove, refrigerator, and microwave is necessary if you enjoy cooking. Similarly, some travelers—especially those who are doing lengthy trips—might not be able to compromise on having a bathroom with a shower and toilet.

It's essential to consider the RV's general condition in addition to the amenities onboard. Make sure to carefully check the car for any indications of wear, damage, or mechanical problems whether you're buying or renting. Examine the RV's age, mileage, and maintenance history carefully. RVs that are kept up properly are less likely to experience unforeseen malfunctions or breakdowns while you are traveling. Before making a purchase, make sure to request maintenance records and think about hiring a professional inspector.

To improve your camping experience, you'll need to spend money on necessary gear and accessories in addition to the RV itself. Having enough power sources is essential for charging electronics and operating appliances when camping. While most RVs have a generator and batteries, you might consider adding solar panels or more batteries for off-grid travels. Additionally, you must have the proper power cords and adapters to connect your RV to different campground electrical hookups.

Managing sewage and water is yet another essential component of RV camping. To fill the freshwater tank in your RV and connect to the campground's water supplies, you'll need fresh water hoses and a water pressure regulator. In addition, to properly empty the wastewater tanks in your RV, you'll need a sewer hose along with the appropriate attachments. Remember to spend money on stabilizers and leveling blocks of the highest caliber to guarantee your RV rests comfortably and securely at your campsite.

Awnings or portable shade structures can significantly improve your outdoor living space in terms of comfort and convenience. These let you take in the natural beauty of the National Parks while remaining comfortable by offering shade and weather protection. Outdoor seating arrangements, like tables and chairs, enhance your campsite's pleasure and tranquility.

Prioritizing safety above all else means ensuring your RV is outfitted with the necessary safety equipment. This includes a fully stocked first-aid kit, smoke and carbon monoxide detectors, and fire extinguishers. Additionally, you can steer clear of low-clearance obstructions and narrow roads that might not be appropriate for your RV by purchasing a high-quality GPS navigation system, especially for RVs.

In conclusion, selecting the ideal RV and gear for your trip through the National Parks is an important choice that needs serious thought. Your trip will be pleasant, safe, and comfortable if you choose the right kind and size of RV, assess its amenities and condition, and purchase necessary gear and accessories. You can fully enjoy the benefits of RV camping and immerse yourself in the breathtaking beauty of the National Parks by taking the time to make informed decisions.

Selecting National Parks to visit

Selecting the right National Parks to visit for an RV trip is a pivotal decision that can profoundly impact your overall travel experience. The United States boasts diverse National Parks, each with unique natural wonders, ecosystems, and recreational opportunities. Therefore, carefully considering your interests, preferences, and travel goals is essential when planning your RV adventure.

First and foremost, you should reflect on your interests and the type of experiences you seek. Are you captivated by the rugged grandeur of mountain landscapes, the tranquility of coastal vistas, or the lush beauty of forests and waterfalls? Understanding your preferences can help you narrow your choices and select National Parks that align with your passions.

Consider the season in which you plan to travel. National Parks can offer vastly different experiences depending on the time of year. Some parks are renowned for their winter wonderlands, where you can engage in activities like snowshoeing and cross-country skiing, while others come alive with vibrant wildflowers and wildlife during the spring and summer months. Research the climate and seasonal highlights of your chosen parks to make the most of your visit.

Accessibility is another crucial factor when selecting National Parks for your RV trip. While many parks offer RV-friendly campgrounds and roadways, others may have limitations due to narrow, winding roads or low-clearance tunnels. Be sure to check the park's official website or contact the park ranger's office for detailed information on RV accessibility, including any size restrictions or recommended routes.

Budget considerations should also be taken into account. Some National Parks charge entrance, camping, or permit fees for certain activities. Create a travel budget that accounts for these expenses and any additional costs associated with RV camping, such as campground reservations, fuel, and supplies. Some parks offer annual passes that provide access to multiple parks, potentially saving you money if you plan to visit several.

Next, consider the activities and experiences you want to enjoy during your RV trip. Are you an avid hiker, birdwatcher, or wildlife enthusiast? Some parks are renowned for their hiking trails, while others offer exceptional birdwatching opportunities or chances to spot elusive wildlife like grizzly bears or wolves. Research each park's specific activities and attractions to ensure they align with your interests.

The duration of your RV trip is another critical consideration. Some National Parks are vast and require several days or even weeks to explore fully, while others can be enjoyed in a shorter timeframe. Determine how much time you have available for your journey and plan your park selections accordingly. Remember that a more extended trip may allow for a more leisurely pace and the opportunity to delve deeper into the natural wonders of each park.

Traveling with companions or family members? It's essential to consider their interests and preferences as well. Engage in open discussions to ensure that everyone's expectations and desires are considered when choosing National Parks to visit. Compromising and finding parks that offer a variety of activities can lead to a more enjoyable and harmonious travel experience.

One vital aspect to remember is the importance of responsible tourism and conservation. Some National Parks are more fragile and sensitive to human impact than others. Research and adhere to park regulations, stay on designated trails, and practice Leave No Trace principles to minimize your environmental footprint and help preserve these pristine natural landscapes for future generations.

In conclusion, selecting the right National Parks to visit for an RV trip requires thoughtful consideration of your interests, preferences, travel goals, and practical factors like accessibility and budget. By conducting thorough research and aligning your choices with your passions and travel companions' needs, you can create a memorable and fulfilling RV adventure through the awe-inspiring beauty of America's National Parks. Whether you seek the majesty of the mountains, the coast's serenity, or the forests' enchantment, there's a National Park waiting to inspire and captivate you on your RV journey.

Booking campsites and permits

Booking campsites and obtaining permits for your RV trip are pivotal to ensuring a smooth and enjoyable journey through national parks and other scenic destinations. The process of securing accommodations and permits can vary significantly from park to park, but understanding the general principles and planning ahead will help you navigate this crucial step of your adventure.

First and foremost, it's essential to research the specific requirements and reservation systems for the National Parks you intend to visit. Many popular parks have high demand for campsites, especially during peak seasons, and booking in advance is often necessary to secure your spot. The National Park Service (NPS) operates an online reservation system for many campgrounds, allowing you to check availability and make reservations well in advance of your trip.

When planning your RV trip, consider the season in which you intend to visit, as this can impact both availability and reservation timelines. Popular parks during the summer months, such as Yellowstone or Yosemite, tend to fill up quickly, sometimes within minutes or hours of the reservation window opening. Be sure to mark your calendar for the opening date of the reservation window for your desired campgrounds and be prepared to book promptly.

Flexibility in your travel dates and campsite choices can be advantageous. If you can travel during off-peak times or explore less-visited areas of National Parks, you may have a better chance of securing reservations even if you miss out on your first choice. Additionally, some campgrounds offer first-come, first-served sites, which can be an excellent option if you arrive early enough to claim an available spot.

Knowing the specific rules and regulations of the National Park you plan to visit is crucial. Different parks have varying policies regarding campsite reservations, length of stay, and permit requirements. Some parks have restrictions on the number of consecutive nights you can camp in one location, while others may require a wilderness permit for backcountry camping or activities like hiking and backpacking. Familiarize yourself with the park's regulations and guidelines to ensure compliance and avoid any unexpected issues during your stay.

Budget considerations are also significant when booking campsites for your RV trip. In addition to the camping fees, you should factor in the cost of entrance fees to the National Park, which are typically separate from camping fees. Some parks offer annual passes granting access to multiple parks, providing potential cost savings if you visit several destinations during your journey.

When reserving campsites for your RV, be prepared to provide specific information about your vehicle's size and amenities. RV campsites often vary in size and suitability for different types of RVs, so accurate details about your RV's length, height, and any additional equipment (such as slide-outs or awnings) are essential to ensure a compatible campsite. Overestimating the size of your RV when making reservations is a wise approach to avoid any complications upon arrival.

For National Parks that do not offer online reservations or have limited availability for larger RVs, it's advisable to contact the park directly or visit their official website for information on campsite availability and reservation procedures. Sometimes, you may need to physically visit the park's visitor center to secure a campsite, especially in remote or less-visited areas.

Permits for specific activities within National Parks, such as hiking in the backcountry or participating in guided tours, may also be required. These permits often have limited quotas and specific application processes. Suppose you plan to engage in activities that require permits. In that case, it's essential to research the availability, application timelines, and any associated fees to ensure you can participate in your desired experiences during your RV trip.

In conclusion, booking campsites and obtaining permits for your RV trip through National Parks requires careful planning, attention to reservation windows, and compliance with park regulations. By researching the requirements and booking procedures for your chosen destinations, remaining flexible when possible, and budgeting for camping and entrance fees, you can streamline the process and ensure a memorable and hassle-free journey. Navigating the complexities of campsite reservations and permits is an essential step that paves the way for an enriching and immersive experience in the natural beauty of America's National Parks. Whether you seek adventure in the wilderness or serenity in the great outdoors, proper planning and preparation will help you make the most of your RV adventure.

Creating a travel itinerary

Creating a travel itinerary for an RV trip is a pivotal step in ensuring a well-organized and enjoyable journey. Your itinerary serves as a roadmap, guiding you through the National Parks and other destinations you plan to explore. It allows you to maximize your time, prioritize your must-see attractions, and make the most of your RV adventure. Here, we'll delve into the key considerations and steps to craft an effective travel itinerary for your RV trip.

The first and foremost consideration in creating your RV travel itinerary is the selection of your destinations. As discussed earlier, choosing the right National Parks and scenic spots that align with your interests and preferences is crucial. Once you have your list of destinations, you can begin to outline the order in which you'll visit them. Consider factors such as proximity, driving distance, and seasonal variations in weather and activities. Organizing your itinerary geographically can help minimize unnecessary driving and maximize your time at each location.

Determine the duration of your RV trip. How many days or weeks do you plan to be on the road? This will play a significant role in shaping your itinerary. Ensure you allocate enough time at each destination to explore its highlights and engage in your chosen activities. Be realistic about travel times between locations, as driving in an RV can be slower than in a regular car, especially on winding or mountainous roads.
Reserving campsites and accommodations is a critical part of your itinerary. As discussed previously, securing campsites in National Parks, especially during peak seasons, can be competitive. Ensure you have reservations for each stop on your itinerary, and double-check the reservation details, including check-in and

check-out times. Some campgrounds have limitations on the length of stay, so plan accordingly.

Plan your daily activities and must-see attractions at each destination. Research the National Park's official website and visitor centers for information on hiking trails, scenic viewpoints, ranger-led programs, and any special events or seasonal highlights. Create a list of activities and sights you want to experience, and allocate time for them in your itinerary. Remember that flexibility is key; unexpected discoveries and opportunities can enhance your RV trip, so leave room for spontaneity.

Factor in downtime and relaxation. While it's tempting to pack your itinerary with activities and sights, remember that RV travel is also about enjoying the journey and the tranquility of your campsite. Allocate some downtime for leisurely mornings, evenings by the campfire, and simply soaking in the natural beauty around you. Balancing adventure with relaxation can lead to a more fulfilling and less stressful RV experience.

Consider your daily travel distances and driving times. RV travel often involves longer driving days, so plan your route to avoid exhausting stretches of road. Aim for a balance between driving and exploration, with occasional shorter travel days to recharge. Be aware of the limitations of your RV, such as fuel range and road conditions, and plan refueling stops accordingly.

Create a packing checklist tailored to your itinerary. Think about the specific gear, clothing, and supplies you'll need for each destination and activity. Different National Parks may have varying climates and terrain, so having the right equipment and clothing is essential. Don't forget to include RV essentials like leveling blocks, hoses, and power cords. Organize your packing list by category to ensure you don't overlook any crucial items.

Stay informed about park hours, entrance fees, and any park-specific regulations. Many National Parks have visitor centers with valuable resources, including maps, brochures, and ranger-led programs. Take advantage of these resources to enhance your experience and stay updated on any park alerts or safety information.

Consider alternative or backup plans. While your itinerary is a blueprint for your trip, unforeseen circumstances like weather, road closures, or campground availability can impact your plans. Having alternative destinations or activities in mind can help you adapt to changing situations without major disruptions to your trip.

Finally, share your itinerary with someone you trust, such as a family member or friend. Provide them with a copy of your travel schedule, contact information, and emergency contacts. This is a precautionary measure to ensure that someone knows your whereabouts and can assist in case of an emergency.

In conclusion, creating a travel itinerary for your RV trip is a vital step that requires thoughtful planning and consideration of your destinations, duration, activities, and logistical details. Crafting a well-organized itinerary enables you to make the most of your RV adventure, ensuring you experience the natural wonders of National Parks while maintaining flexibility and room for relaxation. Whether you're exploring iconic landmarks or venturing off the beaten path, a well-thought-out itinerary is your roadmap to a memorable and fulfilling RV journey.

CHAPTER II

Essential RV Camping Tips

RV maintenance and safety

RV maintenance and safety are paramount considerations for anyone embarking on an RV adventure, especially when planning an extended journey or visiting remote locations. Your RV is not just a mode of transportation; it's your home on wheels, and taking care of it ensures your safety, comfort, and peace of mind throughout your travels.

Regular RV maintenance is essential to prevent breakdowns and ensure a trouble-free journey. Start with a thorough inspection before each trip. Check the engine, tires, brakes, and lights to ensure they are in good working condition. Pay close attention to tire pressure, as underinflated tires can lead to blowouts. Regularly change the oil and perform routine engine maintenance according to the manufacturer's recommendations. A well-maintained engine improves fuel efficiency and reduces the risk of unexpected breakdowns.

Your RV's plumbing system also requires attention. Check for leaks, and make sure all pipes and connections are secure. Use RV-specific toilet paper to prevent clogs in your black water tank. Regularly sanitize your freshwater system to prevent the growth of harmful bacteria. A clean and functional plumbing system ensures your access to essential amenities during your trip.

Electrical systems in your RV should be inspected for safety and functionality. Check all outlets, switches, and appliances for loose connections or signs of damage. Carry spare fuses, bulbs, and electrical components to replace any that may fail during your trip. Consider a surge protector to safeguard against campground power fluctuations, which can damage your RV's electrical systems.

Propane systems are another critical aspect of RV maintenance and safety. Inspect the propane tank, hoses, and connections for leaks or damage. Be cautious when handling propane, as it is highly flammable. Always turn off the propane supply when traveling or when not using appliances that require it. Carbon monoxide detectors and propane gas detectors are essential safety devices in your RV to alert you to potential hazards.

Regularly inspect your RV's exterior, including the roof, windows, and seals. Water intrusion can lead to extensive damage, including rot and mold growth. Ensure that roof seals and seams are well-maintained and reseal them as needed to prevent leaks. Clean and inspect the awnings for signs of wear, and retract them during windy conditions to avoid damage. Check the condition of your windows and seals to prevent drafts and leaks.

A clean and well-maintained interior enhances your comfort and ensures your safety. Regularly clean and sanitize all surfaces to prevent mold and bacteria growth. Check for loose or damaged cabinetry; items can become projectiles during sudden stops or sharp turns. Secure heavy objects, especially when traveling, to prevent accidents.

One of the most critical aspects of RV maintenance is properly caring for your RV's chassis and drivetrain. Regularly inspect the brakes, steering, and suspension for signs of wear or damage. Keep an eye on the condition of your tires, including tread depth and sidewall integrity. Replace tires that show signs of age or damage to prevent blowouts, which can be dangerous and costly.

The RV's brakes should be kept in excellent working order to ensure your safety on the road. Regularly check the brake pads and rotors, and replace them when they show signs of wear. Pay attention to the brake fluid level and top it off as needed to maintain optimal braking performance. Properly functioning brakes are crucial for safe RV operation, especially when navigating steep grades or making sudden stops.

Regularly inspect and maintain your RV's suspension system to ensure a smooth and stable ride. Check the shock absorbers, springs, and bushings for signs of wear or damage. A well-maintained suspension enhances your comfort and contributes to better handling and stability, reducing the risk of accidents or mishaps on the road.

In addition to regular maintenance, safety while driving an RV also involves responsible and cautious driving practices. RVs are larger and heavier than standard vehicles, impacting their handling and braking distances. Take the time to become familiar with how your RV handles, especially in various driving conditions.

Practice defensive driving techniques and maintain a safe following distance from other vehicles. Be mindful of your RV's blind spots, which are more extensive than those of smaller vehicles. Use your side mirrors and, if available, backup cameras to help with navigation and parking. When parking, choose level and stable surfaces to prevent tipping or instability.

Consider taking an RV driving course to improve your skills and confidence behind the wheel. These courses provide valuable insights into RV-specific handling and safety practices, enhancing your ability to operate your RV safely and efficiently.

Another aspect of RV safety is being prepared for emergencies. Equip your RV with a well-stocked first-aid kit, fire extinguisher, and emergency tools such as a flashlight, tire repair kit, and jumper cables. Familiarize yourself with the location and operation of these safety items to quickly respond to unexpected situations.

Furthermore, staying informed about weather conditions and road closures is essential for safe RV travel. Check weather forecasts and road conditions before setting out on your journey. Be prepared for adverse weather conditions, such as rain, snow, or high winds, and adjust your travel plans accordingly. In some cases, it may be safer to delay your trip or seek alternative routes.

It's also wise to have a communication plan in place. Ensure you have a reliable cell phone or satellite phone with you, as well as a list of emergency contacts and roadside assistance services. Share your travel plans and itinerary with someone you trust so that they can assist in case of emergencies.

In conclusion, RV maintenance and safety are critical to ensuring a secure and enjoyable RV journey. Regular maintenance of your RV's engine, plumbing, electrical, and propane systems is essential to prevent breakdowns and hazards. Properly maintaining your RV's chassis and drivetrain contributes to safe handling and braking. Additionally, responsible driving practices, defensive driving techniques, and emergency preparedness are vital components of RV safety. By prioritizing maintenance and safety measures, you can embark on your RV adventure with confidence, knowing that you are well-prepared to navigate the open road and enjoy the natural wonders of your chosen destinations.

Packing essentials for your trip

Packing essentials for your RV trip is crucial in ensuring you are well-prepared for the journey ahead. Unlike traditional travel, where packing space is often limited, an RV offers more room for supplies and gear, making bringing along the essentials you'll need for a comfortable and enjoyable trip easier. Here, we'll delve into the key categories of items you should consider packing for your RV adventure.

First and foremost, think about your kitchen and dining essentials. Your RV likely has a kitchen area, so stock it with cookware, utensils, plates, bowls, glasses, and cutlery. Don't forget essentials like pots, pans, a coffee maker, and a toaster. Consider bringing a portable grill or campfire equipment for outdoor cooking. Ensure you have food storage containers, zip-top bags, and aluminum foil for leftovers and meal prep.

Food and pantry supplies are also vital. Plan your meals and bring along the ingredients you'll need. Non-perishable items like canned goods, pasta, rice, and spices are convenient staples. Don't forget to pack essentials like cooking oil, condiments, and your favorite snacks. Consider a well-stocked pantry to reduce the need for frequent grocery stops, especially when traveling through remote areas.

Bedding and linens are essential for a good night's sleep in your RV. Pack sheets, blankets, and pillows for comfort. Consider extra blankets for chilly nights. Bring towels, washcloths, and kitchen towels for personal use and cleaning.

Personal items and toiletries should be packed as you would for any trip. Remember to bring enough clothing for various weather conditions and activities. Stock up on toiletries, including soap, shampoo, toothpaste, and toilet paper. Consider a first-aid kit with essential medical supplies for minor injuries.

RV-specific essentials are also crucial. Ensure you have leveling blocks to stabilize your RV, especially when parking on uneven terrain. Sewer hoses and attachments are essential for dumping waste. Invest in water hoses and a water pressure regulator for connecting to campground water supplies. A surge protector can safeguard your RV's electrical system from power fluctuations.

Cleaning and maintenance supplies are necessary to keep your RV clean and well-maintained. Pack cleaning supplies such as brooms, mops, sponges, and cleaning solutions. Consider trash bags, recycling bins, and trash cans for managing waste. Don't forget basic RV maintenance tools like a tire pressure gauge, wrenches, and a flashlight.

Outdoor and recreation gear is essential for enjoying the great outdoors during your RV trip. Bring camping chairs, tables, and a portable grill for picnics and outdoor dining. If you plan to hike, bike, or engage in other outdoor activities, pack the necessary equipment and gear, including hiking boots, bicycles, and fishing gear.
Entertainment options are crucial for downtime. While RV travel offers plenty of opportunities for outdoor adventures, having books, board games, playing cards, or portable electronic devices for movies and music can enhance your experience during quiet evenings or rainy days.
Safety and security should always be a top priority.
Ensure you have a fire extinguisher and carbon monoxide detector inside your RV. Pack an essential toolkit for minor repairs and maintenance. Consider a set of road flares, a portable jump starter, and an essential toolset for emergencies. A good communication device, such as a cell phone or satellite phone, is essential for staying connected and seeking help if needed.
Outdoor comfort and relaxation are equally important.
Enhance your outdoor experience by packing camping chairs, a picnic blanket, and portable shade structures like awnings or canopies. Having a comfortable outdoor space

to relax in can significantly enhance your enjoyment of the natural surroundings.

Navigation and maps should not be overlooked. While modern GPS technology is useful, it's wise to have physical maps and navigation tools as backup, especially when exploring remote areas where GPS signals may be weak or unreliable. Paper maps can provide valuable information and help you navigate more effectively.

Travel documents and RV manuals are the final pieces of the puzzle. Don't forget essential travel documents such as your driver's license, RV registration, insurance information, and any necessary permits for specific destinations. Carry a copy of your RV's owner's manual or instructions for reference in case you encounter any technical issues.

In conclusion, packing essentials for your RV trip involves carefully planning and considering the items you'll need for a comfortable and enjoyable journey. Remember to customize your packing list based on your destination, activities, and personal preferences. A well-prepared RV allows you to confidently embark on your adventure, knowing you have everything you need for a memorable and stress-free trip. Whether you're seeking outdoor adventures, relaxation, or a combination of both, thorough packing ensures you can fully embrace the RV lifestyle and make the most of your travels.

Cooking and dining in an RV

Cooking and dining in an RV is a unique and enjoyable aspect of the RV lifestyle. It offers the freedom to prepare your meals while on the road, allowing you to savor delicious dishes and customize your dining experience. However, cooking and dining in the confined space of an RV require thoughtful planning, organization, and some adjustments to your culinary routine.

RV kitchens come in various sizes, from compact galley-style kitchens to more spacious layouts in larger RVs. Your kitchen's size and equipment will dictate your cooking options. Typically, an RV kitchen includes a stove or cooktop, a small refrigerator, a microwave, and a sink. Some may also have a convection oven or a compact dishwasher. It's essential to familiarize yourself with the appliances and equipment in your RV kitchen, as they may differ from what you're used to in a traditional kitchen.

Meal planning is crucial for successful RV cooking. Before your trip, plan your meals and create a shopping list. Consider easy-to-prepare recipes that require minimal cooking time and ingredients. Opt for one-pot or one-pan dishes that reduce the need for multiple pots and pans in your limited kitchen space. Crockpot and instant pot cooking can also be convenient, as they allow you to set and forget your meal while you explore your destination.

Stock up on essential provisions and supplies before hitting the road. Non-perishable items like canned goods, pasta, rice, and spices are convenient staples. Don't forget cooking oil, condiments, and your favorite snacks. Ensure you have food storage containers, zip-top bags, and aluminum foil for leftovers and meal prep. Consider bringing a variety of utensils, pots, and pans suitable for different cooking techniques.

Many RVers enjoy outdoor cooking as part of the RV experience. Consider packing a portable grill or campfire equipment for cooking outdoors. Grilling adds a fun and flavorful dimension to your meals, allowing you to barbecue burgers, steaks, vegetables, and more. Just be sure to follow campground regulations regarding open flames and outdoor cooking.

Safety is paramount when cooking in your RV. Always use appliances and equipment as directed in the manufacturer's instructions. Be cautious when using the stove or cooktop, as RVs can be subject to movement, potentially leading to spills or accidents. Secure pots and pans to prevent them from shifting during travel. Keep a fire extinguisher in your RV's kitchen area, and ensure it's easily accessible in case of emergencies.

When grocery shopping during your RV trip, be mindful of storage limitations in your RV refrigerator and pantry. Consider buying perishable items in smaller quantities and shopping more frequently to ensure freshness. Keep an eye out for local markets and specialty stores in the areas you visit, as they can provide unique culinary experiences and fresh, regional ingredients.

Managing waste is an essential part of RV cooking and dining. Be mindful of food scraps and trash, as RV storage space is limited. Use trash bags and recycling bins to separate waste, and dispose of them following campground rules. Be environmentally responsible by minimizing food waste and using reusable containers and utensils whenever possible.

RV dining can be a delightful experience. Create a cozy atmosphere by setting the table with placemats, utensils, and dishware. Consider using colorful and unbreakable dishes and glassware designed for RV use. Embrace the opportunity to dine al fresco when weather permits, enjoying meals at your campsite's picnic table or under your RV's awning.

One of the joys of RV travel is sampling local cuisine. Explore the culinary traditions of the regions you visit by dining at local restaurants, food trucks, and markets. Don't miss the chance to savor regional specialties and flavors. Engaging with the local food scene is integral to the RV adventure and can lead to memorable dining experiences.

RVers often have a strong sense of community, and sharing meals with fellow campers can be a delightful part of the experience. Consider hosting potluck dinners or campfire cookouts with your neighbors at the campground. Sharing recipes and stories around the campfire can create lasting connections and enrich your RV journey.

In conclusion, cooking and dining in an RV offer a unique and enjoyable aspect of the RV lifestyle. While the compact kitchen space and limited equipment may require some adjustments to your culinary routine, proper planning and organization can ensure you enjoy delicious meals on the road. Embrace the opportunity to explore regional cuisines and engage with fellow RVers in communal dining experiences. Cooking and dining in your RV can enhance your overall travel experience, allowing you to savor the freedom and flexibility of life on the open road while indulging in your favorite dishes.

Managing waste and conservation

Recreational Vehicle (RV) trips offer a unique and exciting way to explore the beauty of the great outdoors while enjoying the comforts of home on wheels. However, these journeys can also generate a significant amount of waste and consume valuable resources if not managed responsibly. In this section, we will delve into the importance of managing waste and conservation during RV trips, highlighting the environmental impact and how individuals can take steps to minimize their ecological footprint.

First and foremost, it is crucial to acknowledge that RVs, while providing comfort and convenience, are not exempt from environmental concerns. They are equipped with various systems, including plumbing, electricity, and waste disposal, which require careful attention to ensure sustainable use. One of the primary areas of concern is freshwater consumption. RVs rely on freshwater tanks for drinking, cooking, and bathing. Excessive water use depletes this precious resource and increases the generation of greywater, which contains soaps and detergents harmful to aquatic ecosystems. To address this, RV travelers should practice water conservation by fixing leaks, using low-flow fixtures, and limiting shower times.

Waste management is another vital aspect of responsible RV travel. RVs come equipped with holding tanks for both blackwater (sewage) and greywater. Improper disposal of these wastes can have detrimental effects on the environment. Dumping sewage directly onto the ground or into water bodies is illegal and poses a severe risk to public health and ecosystems. Therefore, RV enthusiasts must adhere to campground rules and use designated dumping stations to dispose of their waste properly. Furthermore, using environmentally friendly and biodegradable products in RV toilets and sinks can minimize the ecological impact of waste disposal.

Energy conservation is also a key consideration during RV trips. Many RVs are equipped with generators and solar panels to provide electricity, but the excessive use of these resources can contribute to air and noise pollution. Travelers can reduce their carbon footprint by utilizing solar power when available and minimizing generator use. Additionally, LED lighting and energy-efficient appliances can significantly reduce energy consumption within the RV.

While enjoying the beauty of nature during RV trips, it is essential to respect and protect the environment. This includes practicing Leave No Trace principles, which encourage travelers to leave natural areas as they found them. RV enthusiasts should avoid disturbing wildlife and littering and stay on designated paths to prevent soil erosion. By adhering to these principles, travelers can ensure that the pristine wilderness they enjoy remains unspoiled for future generations.

Furthermore, RV travelers should be conscious of their carbon emissions. Although RVs are more fuel-efficient than many other forms of travel, they still emit greenhouse gases that contribute to climate change. To mitigate this, travelers can plan their routes more efficiently, drive at moderate speeds, and properly maintain their RVs to maximize fuel efficiency. Additionally, offsetting carbon emissions through reforestation or renewable energy projects is a proactive way to reduce the environmental impact of RV travel.

Camping locations also play a crucial role in waste management and conservation efforts. Choosing eco-friendly campgrounds that prioritize sustainability can make a significant difference. These campgrounds often offer recycling facilities, water conservation measures, and renewable energy sources, making it easier for RV travelers to minimize their ecological footprint. Researching and selecting such campgrounds can contribute to a more responsible and environmentally friendly RV experience.

In conclusion, managing waste and conservation during RV trips is essential for minimizing the ecological impact of this popular form of travel. RV enthusiasts must be conscious of their freshwater consumption, waste disposal practices, energy use, and carbon emissions. By adopting eco-friendly behaviors, such as water conservation, responsible waste disposal, energy efficiency, and Leave No Trace principles, travelers can enjoy the beauty of the natural world while preserving it for future generations. Additionally, choosing eco-friendly campgrounds can further enhance the sustainability of RV trips. With these considerations in mind, RV travel can continue to be a source of adventure and relaxation while contributing to a healthier planet.

CHAPTER III

Grand Teton National Park

Overview of Grand Teton National Park

Nestled in the rugged terrain of western Wyoming, Grand Teton National Park stands as a testament to the natural beauty and pristine landscapes that define the American West. This national park covers over 300,000 acres and is renowned for its majestic mountain range, pristine lakes, abundant wildlife, and rich human history. In this section, we will embark on a journey through Grand Teton National Park, exploring its geological wonders, ecological diversity, recreational opportunities, and the preservation of its cultural heritage.

The focal point of Grand Teton National Park is undoubtedly the Teton Range, a magnificent mountain range that stretches for approximately 40 miles. Dominated by the imposing peaks of Grand Teton, Mount Owen, and Teewinot, these jagged mountains are a sight to behold. Rising abruptly from the valley floor, the Teton Range is the result of intense geological forces, including faulting and glacial activity, which have sculpted the landscape over millions of years. The park's namesake, the Grand Teton, stands at 13,775 feet, making it the tallest peak in the range and a challenging goal for mountaineers worldwide.

Grand Teton National Park is a haven for geologists and a sanctuary for diverse ecosystems. The park's varied topography, from alpine meadows to dense forests and serene lakes, provides habitat for an impressive array of wildlife. Elk, mule deer, moose, and bison roam the valleys, while black bears, grizzly bears, and gray wolves inhabit the forests. Birdwatchers can spot peregrine falcons, bald eagles, and trumpeter swans in the skies and waters of the park. The park's diverse ecosystems make it a vital part of the Greater Yellowstone Ecosystem, one of Earth's largest and most intact temperate-zone ecosystems.

A network of pristine lakes enhances the natural beauty of the park. Jenny Lake, String Lake, and Leigh Lake are among the most iconic and accessible. Jenny Lake, in particular, is a popular destination for hiking, with its crystal-clear waters reflecting the towering peaks of the Teton Range. These lakes provide stunning vistas and opportunities for fishing, canoeing, and kayaking, allowing visitors to connect with the park's aquatic environments.

The recreational opportunities within Grand Teton National Park are as diverse as its landscapes. Hiking trails crisscross the park, offering adventures for all skill levels. From leisurely strolls along the shores of Jackson Lake to strenuous ascents of the Teton peaks, there's a trail for every hiker. Backpackers can explore the park's remote wilderness areas, while climbers can challenge themselves on the sheer granite faces of the Teton Range. In winter, the park transforms into a wonderland for snow enthusiasts, with cross-country skiing, snowshoeing, and snowmobiling opportunities.

Camping is another popular activity within the park. Grand Teton National Park offers a range of campgrounds, from primitive sites to fully equipped facilities. Camping in the park allows visitors to immerse themselves in the natural surroundings and witness breathtaking sunrises and sunsets against the backdrop of the Teton peaks. However, due to its popularity, campers are advised to make reservations well in advance, especially during the peak summer months.

Beyond its geological and ecological wonders, Grand Teton National Park also tells the story of human interaction with the land. The park is home to numerous historical structures, including the rustic cabins and lodges of the early 20th century. The Moulton Barns in the park's historic district are iconic symbols of the region's pioneering spirit. The park's cultural heritage is also reflected in the presence of Native American archaeological sites, showcasing the long history of human habitation in the area.

Preservation is at the heart of Grand Teton National Park's mission. Its establishment in 1929 and subsequent expansion has been driven by the need to protect and conserve the unique natural and cultural resources within its boundaries. The park's dedicated rangers and staff work tirelessly to ensure the park's delicate ecosystems are preserved for future generations. Conservation efforts extend to managing human impacts, wildlife protection, and ongoing research to better understand and protect the park's biodiversity.

In conclusion, Grand Teton National Park is a testament to nature's grandeur and the preservation of America's wild places. Its majestic mountains, pristine lakes, diverse wildlife, and rich human history make it a destination that captivates the hearts of millions of visitors each year. Whether you're an avid hiker, a wildlife enthusiast, or simply seeking solace in the beauty of the natural world, Grand Teton National Park offers an unparalleled experience that celebrates the wonders of the American West and the importance of preserving our natural heritage for generations to come.

Must-see attractions and hikes

Grand Teton National Park, located in the heart of the Rocky Mountains in Wyoming, is a natural wonderland that beckons adventurers and nature enthusiasts alike.

With its dramatic mountain landscapes, pristine lakes, and abundant wildlife, the park offers many must-see attractions and hikes that showcase the best of this wilderness paradise.

One of the most iconic and visually stunning features of Grand Teton National Park is the Teton Range itself. Towering peaks dominate the skyline, including the Grand Teton, Mount Owen, and Teewinot. The Grand Teton, at 13,775 feet, is the highest peak and a challenging objective for mountaineers. Even for those who don't aspire to summit these peaks, simply gazing at their majesty from viewpoints like Schwabacher Landing or Snake River Overlook is an awe-inspiring experience. The early morning and late evening light often bathes the mountains in a warm, golden hue, making for perfect photography opportunities.

Jenny Lake is another jewel in the park's crown. Lush forests and the towering Teton Range surround this serene, crystal-clear lake. Visitors can take a scenic boat ride across the lake to access various hiking trails or simply enjoy a leisurely stroll along the shore. Hidden Falls and Inspiration Point are popular destinations on the Jenny Lake Trail, offering stunning vistas and the soothing sounds of cascading water.

String Lake, adjacent to Jenny Lake, is another must-visit destination. Known for its tranquil waters and reflections of the Teton peaks, String Lake is a favorite spot for kayaking, canoeing, and paddleboarding. The String Lake Loop Trail provides an easy and scenic hike that encircles the lake, allowing hikers to soak in the serene beauty of the surroundings.

The hike to Amphitheater Lake is a top choice for those seeking a more challenging adventure. This trail takes you through dense forests and open meadows before culminating at the pristine Amphitheater Lake, nestled beneath the imposing Grand Teton. The rugged beauty of the terrain and the stunning alpine lake make this hike a memorable experience for seasoned hikers.

Cascade Canyon, accessible via a boat ride across Jenny Lake, is another hiking gem. The trail winds through a glacially carved canyon, offering breathtaking views of the Tetons and the chance to spot wildlife such as moose and black bears. The trail can be extended to reach Lake Solitude, a remote and peaceful alpine lake surrounded by rugged peaks.

Wildlife enthusiasts will find no shortage of opportunities to observe Grand Teton National Park's diverse fauna. Oxbow Bend on the Snake River is a prime location for wildlife viewing, especially in the early morning and late evening hours. Here, you may spot moose, elk, bison, and various waterfowl. Be sure to have your camera ready to capture these magnificent creatures in their natural habitat.

The Laurance S. Rockefeller Preserve is a unique and tranquil area within the park. It offers a network of trails that wind through lush forests and alongside clear mountain streams. The preserve is a serene oasis, perfect for birdwatching, contemplation, and reconnecting with nature.

Grand Teton National Park also boasts a rich human history that can be explored at the Mormon Row Historic District. This area showcases well-preserved homesteads and barns from the early 20th century, providing insight into the pioneer spirit of the region. The iconic Moulton Barns, with the Teton Range as a backdrop, are a popular subject for photographers and a symbol of the park's cultural heritage.

As you explore the park's attractions and hikes, it's essential to remember the principles of Leave No Trace. Respect the natural environment, pack out all trash, and stay on designated trails to minimize your impact on this pristine wilderness.

In conclusion, Grand Teton National Park is a treasure trove of natural beauty, outdoor adventure, and cultural heritage. Its must-see attractions, from the towering Teton Range to the serene lakes and abundant wildlife, offer visitors a diverse range of experiences. Whether you're a hiker seeking challenging trails, a photographer in search of stunning vistas, or a nature lover hoping to spot wildlife, Grand Teton National Park has something to captivate and inspire everyone who sets foot in its breathtaking landscapes.

RV camping options and recommendations

Grand Teton National Park's stunning landscapes, pristine lakes, and abundant wildlife is a dream destination for RV enthusiasts. Camping within the park allows you to immerse yourself in the Tetons' natural beauty while enjoying your RV's comforts. In this section, we will explore the RV camping options available in Grand Teton National Park and provide recommendations for a memorable RV camping experience.

The park offers several campgrounds that accommodate RVs of varying sizes. Colter Bay RV Park, situated near the northern end of Jackson Lake, is one of the most popular options for RV campers. It provides full hookups, including water, electricity, and sewer, making it ideal for those who prefer modern amenities. The proximity to Jackson Lake and the Colter Bay Visitor Center, which offers informative exhibits and ranger programs, adds to the appeal of this campground.

Another option for RV campers is Gros Ventre Campground, located on the park's eastern side. This campground offers a mix of RV sites with and without hookups, allowing campers to choose based on their preferences. The Gros Ventre River, which runs adjacent to the campground, provides a picturesque backdrop for your RV adventure. Wildlife, including elk and bison, can often be spotted in the surrounding meadows.

Signal Mountain Campground, perched on the shores of Jackson Lake, is another excellent choice for RV camping. This campground offers a range of RV sites, some with electric hookups. The highlight of Signal Mountain Campground is its stunning lake views, particularly at sunrise and sunset. The Signal Mountain Lodge nearby provides dining options and a marina for water activities on Jackson Lake.

For a more rustic RV camping experience, consider Headwaters Campground at Flagg Ranch, which lies just south of Grand Teton National Park. This campground offers a peaceful setting and is an excellent base camp for exploring both Grand Teton and Yellowstone National Parks. While it provides limited hookups, it offers a serene and remote atmosphere surrounded by forests and streams.

While RV camping in Grand Teton National Park offers many conveniences, there are essential considerations to ensure a smooth and enjoyable experience. First, reservations are highly recommended, especially during the peak summer months when the park has the most visitors. You can make reservations through the National Recreation Reservation System.

Proper waste disposal is crucial when RV camping. Most campgrounds within the park provide dump stations for your convenience. Please use them to dispose of blackwater and greywater responsibly. Additionally, using environmentally friendly and biodegradable products in your RV's plumbing system can help minimize your ecological footprint.

Given the popularity of RV camping in Grand Teton National Park, planning your trip well in advance is advisable. The park's campgrounds fill up quickly; last-minute availability can be scarce. Be sure to check the park's website or contact the visitor center for the most up-to-date information on campground availability and reservation procedures.

During your RV camping adventure, take the time to explore the park's natural wonders and recreational opportunities. Grand Teton National Park offers an extensive network of hiking trails, catering to all skill levels. Whether you're seeking a leisurely stroll along the shores of Jackson Lake or a challenging hike to an alpine lake high in the Tetons, there's a trail for you. Be sure to carry bear spray and know how to use it, as the park is home to both black bears and grizzly bears.

Water enthusiasts will find plenty to do in the park's pristine lakes. Canoeing, kayaking, and paddleboarding are popular activities on Jackson Lake and Jenny Lake. Fishing is another favorite pastime, with opportunities to catch cutthroat trout and other native species. Be sure to obtain the required permits and adhere to fishing regulations.

Wildlife watching is a highlight of any visit to Grand Teton National Park. Bison, elk, moose, and mule deer are frequently spotted in the park's meadows and along the riverbanks. Keep a safe distance from wildlife and use binoculars or telephoto lenses for a closer look. Additionally, the park is a haven for birdwatchers, with the chance to spot bald eagles, ospreys, and a variety of waterfowl.

Consider exploring the neighboring attractions outside the park for a change of scenery. The town of Jackson, Wyoming, offers dining, shopping, and cultural experiences. The Jackson Hole Aerial Tram, which takes you to the top of Rendezvous Mountain, provides panoramic views of the Teton Range and the valley below. The nearby National Elk Refuge also offers opportunities to observe a wintering herd of elk up close.

In conclusion, RV camping in Grand Teton National Park offers a unique opportunity to immerse yourself in the natural beauty of the Tetons while enjoying the comforts of your home on wheels. With a variety of campgrounds to choose from, ranging from full hookups to more rustic options, there's something for every RV enthusiast. By making reservations, practicing responsible waste disposal, and taking advantage of the park's recreational opportunities, you can ensure a memorable and enjoyable RV camping experience in this breathtaking wilderness.

Local wildlife and photography tips

With its stunning landscapes and diverse ecosystems, Grand Teton National Park is a haven for wildlife enthusiasts and photographers alike. From the iconic megafauna to the smallest birds, the park offers many opportunities to observe and capture the beauty of its local wildlife. This section will explore some of the park's remarkable wildlife residents and provide photography tips to help you make the most of your wildlife encounters.

One of the most iconic and sought-after species in Grand Teton National Park is the American bison, often simply referred to as buffalo. These massive and majestic creatures symbolize the American West and can be found grazing in the park's meadows and grasslands. Bison are best observed during the early morning or late afternoon when they are most active. To photograph them, use a telephoto lens to maintain a safe distance while capturing their impressive size and rugged appearance. Be patient and respectful, as these animals can be unpredictable.

Moose are another highlight of the park's wildlife population. With their striking size and distinctive antlers, moose are a favorite subject for photographers. They are often seen near lakes and rivers, where they feed on aquatic vegetation. Schwabacher's Landing, along the Snake River, is popular for moose sightings and photography. Remember to keep a respectful distance, as moose can be particularly protective of their young.

Elk are a common sight throughout the park, especially in the open meadows and valleys. During the fall rutting season, male elk, known as bulls, engage in dramatic displays of bugling and sparring. This provides excellent opportunities for action shots and capturing the essence of this seasonal spectacle. Long lenses are advisable for photographing elk, as they can be skittish and are often best observed from a distance.

Bald eagles, with their distinctive white heads and impressive wingspans, are the park's most iconic avian residents. They can often be spotted near bodies of water, where they hunt for fish. Oxbow Bend on the Snake River is a prime location for photographing bald eagles, especially in the winter when they gather to feed on fish trapped in the icy waters. A sturdy tripod and a telephoto lens are invaluable for capturing the intricate details of these magnificent birds in flight.

Ospreys are another raptor species commonly seen in the park. They are known for their dramatic dives into the water to catch fish. The Jackson Lake area is a hotspot for osprey sightings, particularly around the marinas and the shores of the lake. To capture their fishing behavior, use a fast shutter speed and continuous shooting mode to catch the moment of the dive.

The park's lakes and rivers also host a variety of waterfowl, including trumpeter swans, Canada geese, and various species of ducks. These birds can provide excellent opportunities to capture reflections in calm waters and experiment with different lighting conditions. Early mornings and late evenings often offer the best lighting for waterfowl photography.

Small mammals, such as ground squirrels and chipmunks, can be found throughout the park's picnic areas and trailheads. While they may not be as grand as the larger wildlife species, they can make for charming subjects, especially for close-up and macro photography. Be sure to have a telephoto lens for larger wildlife and a macro lens or close-up filters for these smaller critters.

Photographing wildlife in Grand Teton National Park requires both patience and ethical consideration. The welfare of the animals and your safety should always come first. Maintain a safe distance from wildlife, use long lenses to avoid disturbing them, and avoid feeding or approaching them. If an animal changes its behavior because of your presence, you are too close. Be mindful of the park's regulations and guidelines for wildlife photography to ensure a respectful and enjoyable experience for both you and the animals.

Regarding photography equipment, it's advisable to have a versatile kit that includes a range of lenses, from telephoto for wildlife to wide-angle for landscapes. A sturdy tripod is essential for capturing sharp images, especially in low-light conditions. Familiarize yourself with your camera's settings and practice using them before your trip to ensure you can quickly adjust to changing situations in the field.

Lastly, remember that the best wildlife photography often requires patience and persistence. Wildlife can be elusive, and capturing that perfect shot may take time. Be prepared to spend hours observing and waiting for the right moment. Additionally, respecting the park's wildlife and natural environment should always be your top priority.

In conclusion, Grand Teton National Park offers a rich tapestry of wildlife and photographic opportunities. From the grandeur of bison and moose to the grace of bald eagles and ospreys, the park's diverse ecosystems provide a wealth of subjects for photographers. By practicing ethical wildlife photography, using the right equipment, and embracing patience, you can capture the beauty and vitality of the park's local wildlife while preserving its natural integrity for future generations to enjoy.

CHAPTER IV

Zion National Park

Overview of Zion National Park

Nestled in the southwestern United States, Zion National Park is a captivating natural wonderland that beckons visitors with its stunning landscapes, awe-inspiring canyons, and rich ecological diversity. This iconic park, located in the state of Utah, is renowned for its towering red rock formations, serene river valleys, and an array of outdoor adventures. In this section, we will embark on a journey through Zion National Park, exploring its geological marvels, unique ecosystems, recreational opportunities, and the importance of preserving this extraordinary wilderness.

The defining feature of Zion National Park is its remarkable geology. The park's landscape is dominated by towering sandstone cliffs, deep canyons, and narrow slot canyons carved by the Virgin River over millions of years. The Zion Canyon, with its sheer walls rising up to 2,000 feet, is the park's most famous formation. This canyon, sculpted by the river's erosive power, offers breathtaking vistas at every turn. Visitors can witness the interplay of light and shadow as the sun traverses the sky, painting the cliffs with a palette of vibrant colors.

Zion National Park is home to one of the most renowned slot canyons in the world, known as "The Narrows." This narrow, winding gorge features towering walls that can be only a few feet apart, with the Virgin River flowing along the canyon floor. Hiking The Narrows is an unforgettable experience, as you wade through the cool waters and marvel at the sculpted sandstone walls rising hundreds of feet above. The play of light in the narrow passages creates an ethereal atmosphere that enchants photographers and nature enthusiasts alike.

The park's geological history is a tale of sedimentary layers, uplift, and erosion. The Navajo Sandstone, found in Zion, dates back to the Jurassic period and is a testament to the passage of time. Erosion by water and wind over millions of years has shaped the sandstone into the magnificent formations seen today. This ongoing geological process continues to carve and redefine the park's features, ensuring its ever-changing beauty.

Beyond its geological wonders, Zion National Park is home to a rich tapestry of ecosystems. The park's diverse elevations, ranging from low desert to high plateaus, create a mosaic of habitats supporting various plant and animal species. Juniper and pinyon pine forests blanket the lower elevations, while ponderosa pines dominate the higher plateaus. Cottonwood and willow trees thrive along the banks of the Virgin River.

Wildlife abounds in Zion, with mule deer, desert bighorn sheep, and rock squirrels being common sights. The park is also home to a healthy population of California condors, one of the world's most endangered birds. Peregrine falcons, golden eagles, and many other bird species grace the skies above the canyons. The park's biodiversity extends underground, with unique creatures inhabiting the dark recesses of its slot canyons and caves.

Recreational opportunities in Zion National Park are as diverse as its landscapes. Hiking is perhaps the most popular activity, with trails ranging from easy strolls to challenging ascents. The park offers something for everyone, from the accessible Riverside Walk to the strenuous hike to Angels Landing, which rewards hikers with panoramic views of Zion Canyon. For a wet and refreshing adventure, tubing or floating down the Virgin River is a popular summer pastime.

Canyoneering is a thrilling way to explore the park's slot canyons and hidden gems. With proper equipment and guidance, adventurers can rappel down cliffs, swim through narrow canyons, and discover secluded oases. Canyoneering permits are required, as this activity demands a higher level of skill and preparation.

Rock climbing is another beloved pursuit in Zion, drawing climbers worldwide. The park boasts various climbing routes, from beginner-friendly to challenging multi-pitch ascents. Climbers can scale the sheer sandstone walls of Zion Canyon or explore the remote backcountry canyons.

Zion National Park is also a paradise for photographers, with its ever-changing light, striking landscapes, and rich biodiversity. Sunrise and sunset provide the most dramatic lighting conditions, casting a warm and ethereal glow on the cliffs and canyons. The soft, diffused light of overcast days can also create stunning photographic opportunities by reducing harsh shadows.

Preservation is at the core of Zion National Park's mission. The park was established in 1919 to protect its unique natural and cultural resources. Efforts are ongoing to conserve the park's ecosystems and maintain its ecological balance. Visitors are encouraged to follow Leave No Trace principles, respect the environment, and minimize their impact on this fragile wilderness.

In conclusion, Zion National Park stands as a testament to the power of nature and the importance of preserving our natural heritage. Its geological wonders, diverse ecosystems, recreational opportunities, and commitment to conservation make it a destination that captivates the hearts of millions of visitors each year. Whether you're a hiker seeking challenging trails, a photographer in search of stunning vistas, or a nature lover hoping to connect with the wild, Zion National Park offers an unparalleled experience that celebrates the beauty of the natural world while emphasizing the need for responsible stewardship of our planet's treasures.

Popular trails and outdoor activities

Zion National Park, located in the heart of southwestern Utah, is a hiker's paradise and a haven for outdoor enthusiasts. With its towering red rock formations, lush canyons, and breathtaking vistas, the park offers many popular trails and outdoor activities that allow visitors to immerse themselves in its awe-inspiring landscapes. In this section, we will explore some of the most beloved trails and outdoor adventures in Zion National Park, highlighting the beauty and diversity of this remarkable destination.

One of the most iconic trails in Zion is the Narrows. This extraordinary hike takes you through the narrowest section of Zion Canyon, where the towering walls come so close together that they block out most of the sky. The trail is the Virgin River, and hikers wade through the water as they make their way upstream. This unique experience offers a combination of breathtaking beauty and a refreshing escape from the desert heat. Be prepared with appropriate gear, such as water-resistant shoes and walking sticks, as much of the hike involves walking through the river. The Narrows can be enjoyed as a short day hike or an extended adventure, depending on how far you choose to explore.

The Angels Landing trail is a must for those seeking a panoramic view of Zion Canyon. This challenging hike is not for the faint of heart, as it involves a steep ascent with sheer drop-offs on both sides of the narrow ridge leading to the summit. The final stretch is a thrilling scramble up a series of switchbacks and chains anchored into the rock. However, the reward at the top is incomparable – a 360-

degree view of the entire canyon, with the Virgin River winding below. Angels Landing is a hike that demands caution, proper footwear, and attention to safety, but the sense of accomplishment and the awe-inspiring vistas make it an unforgettable experience.

Observation Point is another trail that provides a stunning view of Zion Canyon, albeit from a different perspective. This challenging hike offers a higher vantage point than Angels Landing, allowing you to gaze down upon the iconic landmark from above. The hike begins in the valley and ascends a series of switchbacks before reaching the summit. The view from Observation Point showcases the canyon's vastness and provides a unique opportunity to appreciate the intricate details of the rock formations. Zion

National Park offers numerous shorter hikes that are equally rewarding. The Emerald Pools Trail is a family-friendly option that leads to a series of lush, green pools surrounded by hanging gardens. Lower, Middle, and Upper Emerald Pools offer a pleasant escape into the park's oasis-like environments. The Riverside Walk is another easy hike, which takes you along the Virgin River to the entrance of the Narrows and provides beautiful views of the canyon walls.

For those who prefer a leisurely stroll, the Canyon Overlook Trail offers a relatively short hike with a big payoff. This trail leads to a stunning viewpoint that overlooks the Zion-Mount Carmel Highway and provides a glimpse of the surrounding canyons and mesas. It's an ideal spot for sunrise or sunset photography.

Outdoor activities in Zion National Park extend beyond hiking. Rock climbing is a popular adventure, attracting climbers from around the world. The park's towering sandstone cliffs provide a range of climbing opportunities, from beginner-friendly routes to challenging multi-pitch ascents. Climbing in Zion is a thrilling way to experience the vertical world of the canyon walls.

Canyoneering is another exciting activity unique to Zion. With the right equipment and knowledge, adventurers can explore the park's narrow slot canyons, rappelling down cliffs, swimming through water-filled canyons, and discovering hidden oases. Canyoneering offers an intimate and adventurous way to connect with the park's rugged terrain.

Additionally, the Virgin River offers opportunities for tubing and floating during the hot summer months. Floating down the river allows you to relax and take in the stunning scenery while cooling off in the refreshing waters. Remember that water levels can vary, so checking conditions and safety recommendations is essential before embarking on a river adventure.

Photography is a beloved activity in Zion National Park, thanks to its ever-changing light, striking landscapes, and rich biodiversity. Sunrise and sunset provide the most dramatic lighting conditions, casting a warm and ethereal glow on the cliffs and canyons. The soft, diffused light of overcast days can also create stunning photographic opportunities by reducing harsh shadows. With its vibrant red rocks and lush vegetation, Zion offers endless possibilities for capturing the beauty of the natural world.

In conclusion, Zion National Park beckons adventurers and outdoor enthusiasts with its breathtaking trails and diverse recreational opportunities. Whether you're an experienced hiker seeking challenging ascents or a family looking for leisurely walks and serene viewpoints, Zion has something to offer everyone. The park's unique geology, towering cliffs, and lush canyons create a one-of-a-kind outdoor playground where you can connect with nature and experience the wonders of this remarkable destination.

RV campgrounds and facilities

With its dramatic red rock formations and pristine canyons, Zion National Park is a magnet for outdoor enthusiasts and nature lovers. For those who prefer the comforts of their own home on wheels, Zion offers a range of RV campgrounds and facilities that allow visitors to experience the park's beauty while enjoying the convenience of RV camping. In this section, we will explore the RV campgrounds and amenities available within Zion National Park, providing essential information for a comfortable and enjoyable RV camping experience.

Within Zion National Park's boundaries are two main RV campgrounds: the South Campground and the Watchman Campground. The South Campground is located near the park's south entrance and offers a more primitive camping experience. It provides 117 sites suitable for RVs up to 13 feet in length. These sites come equipped with picnic tables and fire pits, but no hookups are available. The South Campground is an excellent choice for those seeking a more rustic experience and a quieter atmosphere.

The Watchman Campground, situated near the visitor center and the town of Springdale, is the more developed RV campground in Zion National Park. It provides 176 sites for RVs up to 19 feet in length and is equipped with electrical hookups, making it a popular choice for RV campers seeking modern amenities. The campground is also within walking distance of the visitor center, shuttle stop, and the Zion Canyon Scenic Drive entrance, making it convenient for exploring the park's attractions.

Both campgrounds in Zion National Park are in high demand, especially during the peak season from March to November. Reservations are strongly recommended and can be made through the National Park Service reservation system. Due to the limited number of RV sites available, booking well in advance to secure your spot, particularly if you plan to visit during the busy summer months is advisable.

While the South Campground offers a more primitive experience, the Watchman Campground provides several amenities to enhance your stay. Restrooms with flush toilets, potable water, and a dump station are available to campers. Picnic tables and fire rings at each site allow you to enjoy outdoor meals and campfires. It's important to note that the park enforces quiet hours, which run from 10:00 PM to 8:00 AM, ensuring a peaceful and respectful atmosphere for all campers.

Proper waste disposal is crucial when RV camping in Zion National Park. Both campgrounds have dump stations for emptying your RV's wastewater tanks. Using these facilities to minimize your environmental impact and help preserve the park's pristine landscapes is essential. Additionally, generators are permitted in designated areas and during specific hours, so be sure to adhere to the park's guidelines regarding generator use.

If you find that both of Zion National Park's campgrounds are fully booked or if you prefer a more secluded and off-the-beaten-path RV camping experience, there are several private campgrounds and RV parks in the nearby town of Springdale. These options often provide full hookups, showers, laundry facilities, and additional amenities to make your stay more comfortable. Springdale is conveniently located just outside the park's entrance, making it a convenient base camp for exploring Zion.

Beyond camping facilities, Zion National Park offers a range of activities and attractions for RV campers. The park's shuttle system provides convenient access to Zion Canyon, where you can explore iconic trails like the Riverside Walk, the Emerald Pools, and the Weeping Rock. The shuttle is designed to reduce traffic congestion within the canyon and protect the environment, making it hassle-free to access the park's main attractions.

Zion National Park offers world-class hiking and canyoneering opportunities for those seeking adventure. Trails like Angels Landing, the Narrows, and Observation Point provide breathtaking views and unforgettable experiences. Canyoneering enthusiasts can explore the park's narrow slot canyons, such as the Subway and Mystery Canyon, with proper permits and equipment.

Photographers will find endless opportunities to capture the park's stunning landscapes, from the vibrant colors of the sandstone cliffs to the soft, diffused light of the slot canyons. Sunrise and sunset are particularly magical times for photography, as the play of light and shadow creates ever-changing compositions.

In conclusion, RV camping in Zion National Park allows you to experience the park's natural beauty and unique landscapes while enjoying the convenience of modern amenities. Whether you choose the South Campground for a more primitive experience or the Watchman Campground for electrical hookups, careful planning and reservations are vital to securing a spot in this popular destination. Zion's breathtaking vistas, world-class hiking, and canyoneering adventures make it an ideal location for RV camping, ensuring a memorable and immersive outdoor experience in one of the most stunning national parks in the United States.

Geology and unique features of the park

Zion National Park, located in southwestern Utah, is a geological wonderland that showcases some of the most captivating and unique features of the American Southwest. This iconic national park is celebrated for its dramatic red rock canyons, towering sandstone cliffs, and intricate slot canyons carved by the forces of nature over millions of years. In this section, we will delve into the fascinating geology and distinctive features of Zion National Park, shedding light on the forces that have shaped this extraordinary landscape.

The foundation of Zion's geology lies in the Navajo Sandstone, a Jurassic-era rock formation that dates back to approximately 180 million years ago. This striking, salmon-colored sandstone is the canvas upon which the park's story unfolds. The Navajo Sandstone was formed from vast sand dune fields in a region that resembled the modern-day Sahara Desert. Over time, these dunes were buried by additional layers of sediment, and the immense pressure and cementation of the sand grains created the solid rock we see today.

The most defining feature of Zion National Park is its intricate network of deep and narrow canyons. These canyons were carved primarily by the Virgin River, a relentless sculptor for millions of years. The river has meandered through the landscape, eroding away sandstone layers to create the spectacular canyons that draw visitors worldwide. The Zion Canyon, often considered the park's centerpiece, is a prime example of this geological masterpiece, with its sheer walls towering up to 2,000 feet above the river.

Slot canyons are another remarkable geological feature found in Zion. These narrow, winding passages, with walls so close together that they often block out the sky, have been shaped by the erosive power of flash floods. The interaction between water and sandstone creates sinuous corridors with sculpted walls that exhibit a range of colors, from deep reds to glowing oranges. Some of Zion's most famous slot canyons include The Narrows, a water-filled slot canyon, and the Subway, characterized by its unique tubular shape.

Erosion continues to be a dominant geological force in Zion National Park. Rainwater and snowmelt, guided by intricate networks of cracks and fractures in the sandstone, continually shape and redefine the landscape. As water flows through these cracks, it erodes the rock, gradually widening and deepening the canyons. Flash floods, though infrequent, play a critical role in this ongoing process, rapidly carrying away sediment and carving new channels.

The park's towering cliffs, known as "hanging gardens," are another fascinating feature created by Zion's geological processes. These cliffs often appear as if they are sprouting lush gardens directly from their vertical surfaces. The hanging gardens are the result of seeping groundwater laden with dissolved minerals. As the water emerges from the rock face and evaporates, it leaves behind deposits of minerals, creating a vibrant tapestry of greenery amidst the stark red rock.

Angels Landing is one of the most iconic geological features in Zion National Park. This towering sandstone formation rises dramatically above the canyon floor and is accessible via a challenging and exhilarating hike. The trail to Angels Landing involves a steep ascent with sheer drop-offs on both sides of the narrow ridge leading to the summit. The final stretch requires hikers to use chains anchored into the rock to navigate the exposed terrain. The view from Angels Landing offers a breathtaking panorama of Zion Canyon, allowing visitors to appreciate the immense scale of the park's geological wonders. Zion's

geological diversity extends to its varied elevations, which range from the low desert floor to the high plateaus. This diversity gives rise to a mosaic of ecosystems and habitats, each supporting a unique array of flora and fauna. Juniper and pinyon pine forests cloak the lower elevations, while ponderosa pines thrive on the higher plateaus. Cottonwood and willow trees flourish along the banks of the Virgin River, creating verdant oases amidst the desert landscape.

Zion National Park's geology is not only a testament to the forces of erosion and time but also a dynamic and ongoing process that continues to shape the landscape. The interplay of water, wind, and geological processes has created a canvas of natural artistry that captures the imagination of all who visit. It reminds us of the ever-evolving beauty and complexity of our planet's geological history.

In conclusion, Zion National Park is a testament to the awe-inspiring power of geology and the intricate processes that have shaped its unique landscape. From the towering cliffs of Zion Canyon to the narrow passages of its slot canyons, the park's geology offers a captivating and ever-changing tableau of natural wonders. Visitors to Zion are given a remarkable opportunity to witness the ongoing work of geological forces and to immerse themselves in a landscape that embodies the grandeur and beauty of the American Southwest.

CHAPTER V

Great Smoky Mountains National Park

Introduction to the Great Smoky Mountains

Nestled along the border between North Carolina and Tennessee, the Great Smoky Mountains National Park stands as an enchanting testament to the beauty and biodiversity of the Appalachian region. As one of the most visited national parks in the United States, the Great Smokies, as they are affectionately called, offer a diverse range of natural wonders, from lush forests and cascading waterfalls to mist-covered mountain peaks. This section serves as an introduction to this extraordinary national park, shedding light on its history, unique features, recreational opportunities, and its vital role in preserving the natural heritage of the southern Appalachian Mountains.

The Great Smoky Mountains National Park encompasses a vast expanse of more than 800 square miles, making it the largest protected area in the eastern United States. The park's name is derived from the bluish haze that often envelops the mountains, resulting from volatile organic compounds released by the region's abundant plant life. This unique natural phenomenon adds to the park's mystique and has inspired countless visitors throughout the years.

The park's history is deeply intertwined with the cultural heritage of the Appalachian region. Before the park's establishment, the Great Smoky Mountains were home to numerous isolated communities that had thrived for generations. In the early 20th century, the idea of preserving the region's natural beauty gained momentum, and efforts to establish the national park began. By the mid-1930s, with support from the federal government and private organizations, the Great Smoky Mountains National Park was officially established on June 15, 1934, making it the first national park in the eastern United States.

One of the most distinctive features of the Great Smoky Mountains National Park is its lush and diverse vegetation. The park is often called the "Salad Bowl of the World" due to the incredible array of plant species. It boasts over 19,000 documented species of living organisms, including an astounding 1,500 species of flowering plants, 140 species of trees, and an abundance of ferns, mosses, and fungi. Notably, the park is home to one of North America's largest and healthiest stands of old-growth temperate deciduous forests.

The park's rich biodiversity extends to its wildlife as well. It provides habitat for many animals, including black bears, white-tailed deer, wild turkey, and red foxes. Additionally, the park is known for its diversity of salamanders, with approximately 30 different species. The park's dark, cool, and moist environments are ideal for these amphibians, making it a global hotspot for salamander diversity.

Visitors to the Great Smoky Mountains National Park are treated to an abundance of recreational opportunities. The park offers more than 800 miles of hiking trails, ranging from easy walks to challenging backcountry routes. Among the most popular hikes is the trek to Clingmans Dome, the park's highest peak at 6,643 feet. A paved path leads to an observation tower offering panoramic views of the surrounding mountains.

Waterfalls are another highlight of the park, with over 2,000 documented within its boundaries. Laurel Falls, accessible via a paved trail, is one of the most visited waterfalls in the park, while Rainbow Falls provides a stunning backdrop for hikers seeking a more challenging trek. Ramsey Cascades, the tallest waterfall in the park, rewards those who embark on the strenuous hike with its impressive beauty.

The Great Smoky Mountains National Park offers several scenic drives for those interested in auto touring. The Newfound Gap Road, which crosses the park from north to south, provides opportunities to witness the park's diverse ecosystems and varying elevations. Cades Cove Loop Road, a favorite among visitors, meanders through a picturesque valley surrounded by mountains and is renowned for its wildlife sightings.

Photographers are drawn to the Great Smokies year-round, each season offering unique beauty. Spring brings blooming wildflowers, while summer provides lush green landscapes. The vibrant colors of fall foliage are a spectacle to behold, and winter offers serene landscapes with frost-covered trees and snowy vistas.

One of the park's most cherished cultural features is the historic buildings and structures found throughout its boundaries. The park contains a wealth of log cabins, barns, churches, and grist mills dating back to the 19th and early 20th centuries. These structures are preserved as a tribute to the Appalachian heritage and offer visitors a glimpse into the past.

The Great Smoky Mountains National Park is vital in scientific research and conservation efforts. Its designation as an International Biosphere Reserve and a UNESCO World Heritage Site underscores its significance in preserving biological diversity and ecological processes. Scientists and researchers continuously study the park's ecosystems, providing valuable insights into the health and sustainability of temperate deciduous forests.

In conclusion, the Great Smoky Mountains National Park is a testament to the southern Appalachian Mountains' enduring beauty and ecological richness. Its diverse landscapes, abundant flora and fauna, and cultural heritage make it a cherished destination for nature lovers, hikers, photographers, and history enthusiasts alike. As one of the crown jewels of the national park system, the Great Smokies continue to inspire and captivate visitors while serving as a vital haven for biodiversity and conservation efforts in the heart of the eastern United States.

Hiking and wildlife experiences

The Great Smoky Mountains National Park, straddling the border between North Carolina and Tennessee, is a haven for outdoor enthusiasts seeking hiking adventures and wildlife encounters. With over 800 miles of hiking trails and a rich biodiversity that includes black bears, white- tailed deer, and many other species, the park offers visitors a chance to immerse themselves in the natural wonders of the southern Appalachian Mountains. This section will explore the hiking opportunities and wildlife experiences that await those who venture into the Great Smoky Mountains.

Hiking in the Great Smoky Mountains National Park is a beloved activity that allows visitors to explore many landscapes, from dense forests and cascading waterfalls to high mountain peaks and serene meadows. The park offers trails suited to hikers of all skill levels, from easy strolls to challenging backcountry adventures.
One of the most iconic and accessible trails in the park is Laurel Falls Trail. This paved path leads to the spectacular Laurel Falls, one of the park's most visited waterfalls. The trail is relatively short, making it ideal for families and those seeking a brief, yet rewarding hiking experience.

Laurel Falls cascades gracefully over 80 feet and provides an excellent photographic backdrop.

The Alum Cave Trail is a popular choice for those looking for a more challenging hike with the promise of stunning vistas. This moderately strenuous trail leads to Alum Cave Bluffs, a unique geological feature that resembles a massive concave ledge. Along the way, hikers are treated to panoramic views of the park, with opportunities to see iconic landmarks like Mount LeConte. The trail's diverse scenery adds to its allure, including rhododendron tunnels and moss-covered rocks.

Clingmans Dome Trail is a must for ambitious hikers and those seeking the highest point in the park. It leads to the summit of Clingmans Dome, the park's highest peak at 6,643 feet above sea level. The trail involves a paved path leading to an observation tower, providing breathtaking 360-degree views of the surrounding mountains. On a clear day, visitors can see for miles, making it an excellent sunrise or sunset photography spot.

The Great Smoky Mountains National Park is renowned for its waterfalls, and Rainbow Falls Trail is a prime example of the park's stunning cascades. This moderately strenuous hike leads to Rainbow Falls, an 80-foot waterfall known for the colorful rainbows that appear in the mist on sunny afternoons. The trail meanders through lush forests and crosses clear mountain streams, offering hikers a refreshing and picturesque journey.

Ramsey Cascades Trail is another hike that takes you to the tallest waterfall in the park, Ramsey Cascades. This challenging hike is known for its steep and rocky terrain, making it a demanding adventure for experienced hikers. However, the reward at the end is the sight of the 100-foot waterfall cascading over moss-covered boulders, surrounded by old-growth forest.

While hiking in the Great Smoky Mountains, being prepared and respecting the environment is essential. Weather conditions can change rapidly, and even in the summer, high elevations can be cool or rainy, so it's advisable to dress in layers and carry essentials like water, snacks, and a map. The park's Leave No Trace principles emphasize responsible hiking practices, including staying on designated trails, packing out trash, and respecting wildlife and other visitors.

The Great Smoky Mountains National Park is a paradise for hikers and a sanctuary for wildlife. The park's diverse ecosystems provide habitat for a remarkable array of species, including black bears, white-tailed deer, wild turkeys, and red foxes. Black bears, in particular, are a symbol of the park and a famous wildlife sighting. While the park does not guarantee bear encounters, the chance of spotting one is relatively high, especially in the Cades Cove area.

The park's biodiversity extends to its amphibians, with nearly 30 different species of salamanders found here. The moist and cool environments of the Great Smokies are ideal for these amphibians, and the park is considered a global hotspot for salamander diversity. Many species are quite small and may go unnoticed by visitors, but they play essential roles in the park's delicate ecosystem.

Birdwatchers also find the Great Smoky Mountains to be a rewarding destination. The park is home to various bird species, from raptors like red-tailed hawks and bald eagles to songbirds like the eastern bluebird and the colorful scarlet tanager. Birdwatching can be enjoyed along the park's trails, open meadows, and various overlooks.

While wildlife encounters in the park can be thrilling, following responsible wildlife viewing guidelines is essential. This includes maintaining a safe distance from animals, not feeding them, and avoiding actions that could stress or disturb them. Respect for wildlife ensures their well-being and helps preserve the natural balance of the park's ecosystems.

In conclusion, the Great Smoky Mountains National Park offers many hiking opportunities and wildlife experiences that allow visitors to connect with the beauty and biodiversity of the southern Appalachian Mountains. Whether you're embarking on a leisurely hike to a waterfall or seeking a challenging ascent to a mountain peak, the park's diverse trails cater to all levels of hikers. And while you explore the trails, keep your eyes peeled for the park's diverse wildlife, from the elusive black bear to the tiny and colorful salamanders. The Great Smoky Mountains National Park is a sanctuary of natural wonder, waiting to be explored and cherished by all who venture within its boundaries.

RV-friendly campgrounds

The Great Smoky Mountains National Park, straddling the border between North Carolina and Tennessee, is a cherished destination for RV enthusiasts seeking to immerse themselves in the beauty of the southern Appalachian Mountains. The park offers a range of RV-friendly campgrounds that provide the perfect base camp for exploring the diverse landscapes, hiking trails, and wildlife experiences the Great Smokies offer. This section will explore the RV-friendly campgrounds within the park, offering valuable information for those planning to embark on an RV adventure in this natural wonderland.

Within the Great Smoky Mountains National Park are several campgrounds suitable for RVs, each with unique features and amenities. It's important to note that while the park welcomes RV campers, some limitations exist, such as size restrictions and a lack of full hookups.

Cades Cove Campground, located in the Cades Cove area of the park, is a favorite among RV campers. It offers both a serene natural setting and the convenience of RV- friendly sites. While the campground doesn't provide hookups for water, sewage, or electricity, it can accommodate RVs up to 40 feet long, making it a suitable choice for many RV owners. Cades Cove is renowned for its wildlife viewing opportunities, with deer, black bears, and turkeys often spotted in the area. The campground is also conveniently situated near the Cades Cove Loop Road, a famous scenic drive.

Elkmont Campground is another option for RV campers in the park. It provides a mix of RV and tent sites, with some sites offering electrical hookups. The campground is situated in a beautiful forested area along the Little River, offering a serene atmosphere. Elkmont is an excellent choice for those looking to explore the park's hiking trails, as it's near the trailheads for popular hikes like Laurel Falls and Alum Cave. The campground can accommodate RVs up to 32 feet in length.

Abrams Creek Campground is a more secluded option within the park, located on the western side near the Abrams Creek area. While it doesn't offer electrical hookups, it can accommodate RVs up to 12 feet long, making it suitable for smaller RVs or trailers. Abrams Creek Campground provides a peaceful setting along Abrams Creek, with opportunities for fishing and access to the Cooper Road Trail. It's an excellent choice for those seeking a quieter camping experience.

The nearby towns outside the park offer private campgrounds and RV parks for RV campers who prefer more amenities, such as full hookups and modern facilities. These options typically provide services like water, electricity, sewage hookups, showers, laundry facilities, and Wi-Fi access. Gatlinburg, Pigeon Forge, and Townsend, Tennessee, are popular gateway towns with private RV campgrounds and amenities, making them convenient bases for exploring the Great Smoky Mountains National Park.

When planning an RV camping trip in the Great Smoky Mountains National Park, one must be aware of some critical considerations. Reservations are recommended, especially during the peak season from spring to fall, as campgrounds can fill up quickly. Reservations can be made through the National Park Service reservation system or by contacting the campground directly. Due to the park's popularity, securing a reservation well in advance is advisable.

Additionally, while the park's campgrounds offer a range of amenities, they do not provide full hookups for RVs. Campers should be prepared to bring their own water, as potable water is typically available in the campgrounds, but not at individual RV sites. Dump stations are available for emptying wastewater tanks, and generators are permitted during specific hours, but it's essential to adhere to the park's guidelines regarding generator use to ensure a respectful and peaceful camping experience for all.

The Great Smoky Mountains National Park is a place of natural wonder, with its lush forests, cascading waterfalls, and diverse wildlife. RV camping within the park allows visitors to fully immerse themselves in this beauty, allowing them to wake up to the sounds of nature and the sight of mist-covered mountain peaks. Whether you camp in one of the park's campgrounds or opt for a private RV park outside the park boundaries, the Great Smoky Mountains offer an RV-friendly experience that celebrates the grandeur of the southern Appalachian Mountains and the importance of preserving this national treasure.

History and cultural aspects of the park

The Great Smoky Mountains National Park, spanning the border between North Carolina and Tennessee, is renowned for its stunning natural beauty and holds a rich history and cultural significance that adds depth to its allure. Established in 1934, the park has been a sanctuary for biodiversity, providing a haven for wildlife and preserving the heritage of the southern Appalachian Mountains. In this section, we will delve into the history and cultural aspects of the Great Smoky Mountains National Park, shedding light on the human stories, traditions, and the enduring legacy of the region.

Before the establishment of the national park, the Great Smoky Mountains were home to numerous isolated communities that had thrived in the region for generations. These hardy settlers, primarily of Scots-Irish descent, carved out a living from the land through subsistence farming, hunting, and crafts. Their way of life was intimately connected to the mountains, and they developed a rich cultural heritage that has left an indelible mark on the park's history.

The early settlers of the Smokies brought with them a deep love for music and storytelling. Appalachian folk music, with its distinctive fiddle and banjo tunes, became a cornerstone of the region's culture. The sound of bluegrass, ballads, and gospel hymns filled the mountain hollows, and musicians like the Carter Family and Ralph Peer helped popularize Appalachian music on a national scale. Today, the park continues to celebrate this musical heritage through events like the Mountain Life Festival, which features traditional music and dance.

Craftsmanship also played a significant role in the cultural history of the region. Isolated communities developed their own distinctive styles of quilting, weaving, and woodworking, passing down these skills through generations. The park's annual Fall Folklore and Mountain Life Festival showcases the work of local artisans who carry on these traditions. Visitors can witness the creation of handmade crafts and learn about the history of Appalachian craftsmanship.

One of the most visible remnants of the region's cultural history is the historic buildings and structures found throughout the park. These cabins, barns, churches, and grist mills date back to the 19th and early 20th centuries and offer a glimpse into the past. Preserving these structures allows visitors to connect with the lives of the early settlers and gain an appreciation for the hardships they endured in the rugged mountain environment. Cades Cove, a popular destination within the park, provides a window into the human history of the Great Smoky Mountains. This picturesque valley was once home to a thriving community of settlers cultivating the fertile land. Today, the loop road that encircles Cades Cove takes visitors past well-preserved historic buildings, including churches, cabins, and a working grist mill. Interpretive programs and exhibits provide insight into the lives of the people who lived in this remote mountain cove.

In addition to the park's cultural history, the establishment of the Great Smoky Mountains National Park itself is a story of collaboration and conservation. The park was established on June 15, 1934, making it the first national park in the eastern United States. Its creation resulted from concerted efforts by individuals, organizations, and government entities at the local, state, and federal levels. John D. Rockefeller, Jr. played a pivotal role in acquiring and donating land for the park, and his contributions were instrumental in its establishment. Preserving the Great Smoky Mountains as a national park was a conservation triumph, as it protected a vast and diverse landscape from the threats of logging and development. The park's designation as an International

Biosphere Reserve and a UNESCO World Heritage Site underscores its significance in preserving biological diversity and ecological processes.

While the natural beauty and recreational opportunities of the Great Smoky Mountains National Park often take center stage, the park's cultural history and human stories add depth and meaning to the visitor experience. The enduring legacy of early settlers, their music, craftsmanship, and the preservation of their historic buildings, offer a unique perspective on the park's rich cultural tapestry. As visitors explore the trails, valleys, and mountains of the Great Smokies, they can connect with the past, gaining a deeper appreciation for the intricate relationship between humans and the natural world in this extraordinary national park.

CHAPTER VI

Yellowstone National Park

Exploring the wonders of Yellowstone

Yellowstone National Park, located primarily in the U.S. state of Wyoming, with portions extending into Montana and Idaho, stands as a natural marvel and a testament to the power of geological forces. Established in 1872, it is the first national park in the world, setting the stage for the conservation of America's natural treasures. Yellowstone's 2.2 million acres encompass a remarkable diversity of ecosystems, geothermal features, wildlife, and landscapes, making it a bucket-list destination for nature enthusiasts and adventurers. In this section, we will embark on a journey to explore the wonders of Yellowstone National Park, shedding light on its unique features, geological phenomena, vibrant wildlife, and the captivating experiences that await its visitors.

One of the most iconic features of Yellowstone National Park is its geothermal wonders, which include geysers, hot springs, mud pots, and fumaroles. The park is home to over half of the world's geysers, with Old Faithful being the most famous among them. Old Faithful regularly erupts with a predictable schedule, making it a must-see spectacle for visitors. The geothermal activity at Yellowstone results from the park's location atop a supervolcano, providing a mesmerizing display of the Earth's inner forces.

Grand Prismatic Spring, located in the Midway Geyser Basin, is another geothermal marvel that captivates with its stunning colors and intricate formations. The spring's vibrant blue center gives way to a gradient of oranges and yellows, surrounded by rings of green, making it the largest hot spring in the United States. The park offers a boardwalk trail that allows visitors to admire this natural wonder from various vantage points.

Yellowstone's geothermal features extend beyond geysers and springs. The Norris Geyser Basin, the hottest and most dynamic in the park, showcases a wide range of geothermal activity. Visitors can explore the Porcelain Basin and Back Basin areas, witnessing geysers' constant change and unpredictability, including Steamboat Geyser, the world's tallest active geyser.

Beyond the geothermal wonders, Yellowstone National Park boasts diverse landscapes, including lush forests, high alpine meadows, cascading waterfalls, and pristine lakes. The Grand Canyon of the Yellowstone is a breathtaking testament to the park's geological history, with its towering waterfalls and colorful rock formations. Artist Point, overlooking the canyon's Lower Falls, provides one of the park's most famous and photographed vistas.

Yellowstone Lake, one of the largest high-elevation lakes in North America, offers a serene and picturesque setting. Mountain peaks surround the lake's crystal-clear waters and provide boating, fishing, and lakeside picnics opportunities. Nearby, the West Thumb Geyser Basin surprises visitors with its geothermal features right along the lake's shoreline.

Hiking is a popular way to explore the varied landscapes of Yellowstone National Park. The park offers over 900 miles of hiking trails that cater to all levels of hikers, from easy walks to challenging backcountry treks. The Fairy Falls Trail is a relatively easy hike that leads to the striking Fairy Falls, surrounded by colorful thermophilic bacterial mats. For those seeking a more challenging adventure, the hike to the summit of Mount Washburn offers sweeping panoramic views of the park's wilderness.

Yellowstone's wildlife is as diverse as its landscapes. The park has various iconic species, including grizzly bears, black bears, gray wolves, bison, elk, moose, and pronghorn. The Lamar Valley, often called the "Serengeti of North America," provides excellent wildlife viewing opportunities, especially for those hoping to spot wolves and bison. Hayden Valley is another prime location for observing bison herds and other wildlife.

The park's commitment to wildlife conservation has led to the successful reintroduction of gray wolves, which had been absent from the region for nearly 70 years. The wolves are thriving today, and their presence contributes to the park's ecological balance.

Yellowstone National Park also offers opportunities for outdoor recreation, including camping, fishing, and horseback riding. The park provides a range of campgrounds, from primitive backcountry sites to developed campgrounds with amenities. Reservations are highly recommended, especially during the peak summer season when the park attracts the most visitors.

For anglers, Yellowstone's rivers and lakes offer excellent fishing for species like cutthroat trout and rainbow trout. Fishing permits are required and can be obtained at park visitor centers. Horseback riding is another enjoyable way to explore the park, with guided rides available at various locations.

In conclusion, Yellowstone National Park is a crown jewel among America's national parks, offering a treasure trove of natural wonders, geological marvels, vibrant wildlife, and outdoor adventures. Its geothermal features, including Old Faithful and Grand Prismatic Spring, provide captivating displays of Earth's inner workings. The park's diverse landscapes, from the Grand Canyon of the

Yellowstone to serene lakes and alpine meadows, offer endless opportunities for exploration and awe-inspiring vistas. And the rich diversity of wildlife, including grizzly bears, wolves, and bison, ensures that every visit to Yellowstone is a wildlife encounter waiting to happen. Yellowstone National Park is a testament to the power and beauty of the natural world, inviting visitors to embark on an unforgettable journey into the heart of this remarkable wilderness.

Geothermal features and geysers

Yellowstone National Park, located primarily in Wyoming but extending into Montana and Idaho, is home to one of the world's most remarkable collections of geothermal features and geysers. These unique natural wonders are a testament to the park's geological history and its location atop a supervolcano. Yellowstone's geothermal landscape is a captivating blend of geysers, hot springs, mud pots, and fumaroles that draw visitors from around the globe. In this section, we will explore the geothermal features and geysers of Yellowstone National Park, shedding light on their formation, significance, and the awe-inspiring experiences they offer to those who venture into this geothermal wonderland.

Yellowstone National Park is situated within the Yellowstone Caldera, a massive volcanic structure created by multiple eruptions over the last two million years. The park's geothermal features directly result from the heat generated by the molten rock, or magma, beneath the Earth's surface. Water from rainfall and snowmelt infiltrates the ground, percolates deep into the Earth's crust, and eventually encounters the superheated rocks below. This process heats the water, causing it to rise back to the surface, where it emerges as hot springs, geysers, and other geothermal phenomena.

One of the most iconic geothermal features in Yellowstone is Old Faithful. It's renowned for its regular eruptions, which occur approximately every 90 minutes, sending boiling water and steam shooting up to 184 feet into the air. This predictable schedule has made Old Faithful a favorite among visitors. While its eruptions are a spectacle to behold, the reliability of Old Faithful is a result of a delicate balance between the size of its underground reservoir, the amount of water, and the pressure buildup.

Grand Prismatic Spring, located in the Midway Geyser Basin, is another highlight of Yellowstone's geothermal wonders. It is the largest hot spring in the United States and boasts brilliant colors created by thermophilic bacteria living in the hot waters. The spring's vivid blue center transitions to a vibrant gradient of oranges and yellows, surrounded by rings of green. The temperature of Grand Prismatic Spring is near boiling, and its depths remain uncharted, adding to its mystique.

The Norris Geyser Basin, the hottest and most dynamic in the park, offers visitors a glimpse into the ever-changing nature of geothermal features. The basin includes the Porcelain Basin and Back Basin areas, showcasing geysers, hot springs, and fumaroles. Among the geysers in Norris is Steamboat Geyser, the world's tallest active geyser. While its eruptions are infrequent and unpredictable, they can reach heights of over 300 feet, creating an awe-inspiring display of nature's power.

Mammoth Hot Springs, located in the northern part of the park, is yet another unique geothermal area. The terraces of Mammoth are formed by the deposition of travertine, a type of limestone, as hot water laden with dissolved calcium carbonate flows over the landscape. Over time, these terraces have created intricate and colorful formations, making Mammoth Hot Springs a fascinating area to explore.

Yellowstone's geothermal features extend beyond the well-known attractions, with countless hot springs, mud pots, and fumaroles scattered throughout the park. Black Sand Basin, Fountain Paint Pots, and the West Thumb Geyser Basin are just a few of the many areas where visitors can witness these fascinating geothermal phenomena. Each feature has unique characteristics, from bubbling mud pots to colorful hot springs, offering diverse experiences.

Yellowstone's geothermal features are captivating to behold and play a crucial role in scientific research and understanding Earth's processes. The park serves as a living laboratory where scientists study extremophiles, microorganisms that thrive in extreme conditions such as high temperatures and acidity. These microorganisms hold significance in fields like microbiology and astrobiology, providing insights into the potential for life on other planets.

While exploring Yellowstone's geothermal wonders, visitors are reminded of the power and unpredictability of the natural world. The park's geothermal features testify to the Earth's dynamic nature and the ever-changing forces that shape the planet's surface. It is essential to exercise caution when visiting these areas, as the scalding waters and thin crust can pose hazards. Visitors are advised to stay on designated trails and boardwalks and to respect safety regulations.

In conclusion, the geothermal features and geysers of Yellowstone National Park are a remarkable testament to the Earth's geological processes and the power of nature. From the iconic eruptions of Old Faithful to the stunning colors of Grand Prismatic Spring, these features offer a glimpse into the Earth's inner workings. Yellowstone's geothermal landscape is a living reminder of our planet's dynamic and ever-evolving nature, and it provides a unique opportunity for visitors to witness the beauty and complexity of the natural world.

RV accommodations and campfire stories

Yellowstone National Park, known for its geysers, hot springs, and vibrant wildlife, offers a unique and unforgettable experience for RV enthusiasts. The park's diverse landscapes and geothermal wonders make it an ideal destination for those seeking to connect with nature while enjoying the comforts of their recreational vehicles. RV accommodations within the park provide a gateway to exploration, offering convenient access to iconic attractions and the opportunity to create campfire stories that will be cherished for years to come. In this section, we will delve into the RV accommodations and the tradition of campfire storytelling in Yellowstone National Park, highlighting the blend of natural beauty and human connection that defines the RV experience in this iconic destination.

Yellowstone National Park provides RV-friendly campgrounds, welcoming visitors to immerse themselves in the park's breathtaking landscapes and geothermal wonders. These campgrounds offer various amenities and experiences, allowing RV travelers to choose the best setting.

Madison Campground near the Madison River is a popular choice for RV campers. It offers RV sites with pull-through and back-in options, suitable for various vehicle sizes. Madison is strategically positioned between the park's western and central regions, providing easy access to iconic attractions like Old Faithful and the Grand Canyon of the Yellowstone. The campground's proximity to the Madison River also makes it a prime spot for fly fishing.

Fishing Bridge RV Park, situated near the Yellowstone River, is the only RV campground within the park that offers full hookups. While it doesn't have the traditional campfire rings due to concerns about bear activity, it provides a convenient base for RV travelers looking for modern amenities. Fishing Bridge is well-positioned for those interested in exploring the park's northern and eastern regions, including the Lamar Valley, known for its wildlife viewing opportunities.

Bridge Bay Campground, also located on the shores of Yellowstone Lake, offers RV sites with beautiful lake views. While it doesn't have full hookups, it provides a serene setting for RV campers looking to enjoy the peacefulness of the lake's expansive waters. The campground is centrally located, making it a great starting point for exploring the park's northern and southern areas.

Grant Village Campground, nestled near the West Thumb of Yellowstone Lake, offers RV sites with varying levels of hookups. It provides a tranquil environment and is close to several geothermal features, including West Thumb Geyser Basin. The campground's lakeside setting offers opportunities for lakeshore walks and water-based activities.

Canyon Campground, situated near the Grand Canyon of the Yellowstone, provides RV campers with a picturesque backdrop for their adventures. It offers RV sites with pull-through and back-in options and is near the park's stunning canyon and waterfalls. The campground's central location makes it a convenient base for exploring Yellowstone's upper and lower loops.

While RV campers can enjoy the comforts of their vehicles, campfires have been a cherished tradition in national parks for generations, allowing visitors to come together, share stories, and connect with the natural world. However, in Yellowstone National Park, campfires are limited to designated fire rings and grates, and firewood must be obtained from park-approved sources to prevent the spread of invasive species and diseases.

The tradition of campfire storytelling is deeply rooted in the park's history, with tales of explorers, early settlers, and Native American tribes weaving a tapestry of human connection to the land. Today, RV campers gather around campfires in the evenings to share their own stories, experiences, and adventures. These gatherings offer a sense of community and camaraderie, allowing travelers from diverse backgrounds to bond over their shared love of nature and exploration.

Campfire stories in Yellowstone often center on the day's adventures, wildlife encounters, and the awe-inspiring geothermal features. The tales told under the starry skies of the park carry the essence of Yellowstone's magic, preserving the memories of encounters with bison, elk, or the rare sighting of a gray wolf. They recount the exhilaration of witnessing Old Faithful's eruption or Grand Prismatic Spring's ethereal beauty.

As the flames flicker and the night settles in, campers might also share stories of Yellowstone's history and significance. The tales of early explorers like John Colter, who ventured into the region in the early 1800s, evoke a sense of wonder about the untamed wilderness that once existed. The cultural heritage of Native American tribes, who have long considered Yellowstone a sacred place, adds depth to the storytelling tradition.

Beyond the natural wonders and historical narratives, campfire stories in Yellowstone often touch on the importance of conservation and stewardship. RV campers share their commitment to preserving the park's pristine landscapes and ensuring that future generations can experience its wonders. These conversations inspire a sense of responsibility and reinforce the connection between visitors and the park's fragile ecosystem.

In conclusion, Yellowstone National Park's RV accommodations offer a gateway to exploration, providing the perfect blend of comfort and immersion in the park's natural wonders. RV travelers can choose from various campgrounds that cater to different preferences, from lakeside serenity to proximity to iconic attractions. While the park's regulations limit the use of campfires to designated areas, the tradition of campfire storytelling remains alive and well among RV campers. These gatherings around the fire offer a sense of community and connection, allowing travelers to share their experiences, marvel at the park's beauty, and reflect on the importance of conservation. In Yellowstone National Park, the combination of RV accommodations and campfire stories creates a unique and memorable experience that celebrates the majesty of nature and the bonds that connect us to this extraordinary destination.

Safety tips for bear encounters

Yellowstone National Park, renowned for its breathtaking landscapes and abundant wildlife, is also home to a healthy population of black bears and grizzly bears. Encounters with these magnificent creatures are a highlight for many visitors, but it's crucial to remember that bears are wild animals and should be treated with respect and caution. Understanding how to navigate bear encounters safely is essential for your safety and the well-being of the bears.

One of the most effective tools for deterring bear encounters is bear spray. It's a form of pepper spray specially designed for use against bears. When hiking in bear country, always carry bear spray, ensure it's easily accessible, and know how to use it. Bear spray is not a substitute for practicing safe bear etiquette.

Bears prefer to avoid encounters with humans, and making noise while hiking can help alert them to your presence. Talk, sing, clap your hands, or use bear bells to make noise as you move through the park. This will help reduce the chances of surprising a bear, which could lead to a defensive reaction.

Whenever possible, hike with at least three or more people. Bears are less likely to approach a group of people than a solitary hiker. Larger groups are generally safer and provide more security in bear country.

Stick to established trails and maintained areas when hiking. Bears are more likely to be encountered in remote or off-trail areas. Staying on designated paths reduces the risk of stumbling upon a bear in its natural habitat.

Always maintain a safe distance from bears and other wildlife. The National Park Service recommends staying at least 100 yards (about the length of a football field) away from bears and wolves and 25 yards from all other wildlife. Use binoculars or a telephoto lens for close-up wildlife viewing.

When camping or picnicking, store all food, cooking equipment, and scented items in the park's bear-resistant food storage containers or lockers. Do not leave food unattended, and avoid cooking near sleeping areas.

Bears are also attracted to trash and human waste. Use designated trash receptacles or dumpsters within the park. When camping, pack out all trash and waste, and use restroom facilities provided by the park.

Be particularly vigilant in areas known to have bear activity. These include backcountry trails, berry patches, and riverbanks. Look for signs of recent bear activity, such as tracks, scat, or fresh diggings.

Understanding bear behavior can help you assess the situation if you encounter one. Bears may exhibit signs of curiosity, nervousness, or agitation. If a bear stands on its hind legs, it is often trying to get a better view and is not necessarily being aggressive.

Under no circumstances should you approach or feed a bear. Maintain a safe distance and use binoculars or a camera with a telephoto lens to observe wildlife. Feeding bears is illegal and dangerous for both bears and humans. If you do encounter a bear, remain calm and avoid sudden movements. Speak calmly and firmly to the bear while slowly backing away. Do not run, as this can trigger a chase response. In the rare event of a charging grizzly bear, lie flat on your stomach with your hands clasped behind your neck and legs spread apart to make it harder for the bear to flip you over.

If you have a bear encounter or witness any bear-related incidents in the park, report them to a park ranger as soon as possible. This information helps park officials monitor bear behavior and ensure visitor safety.

In conclusion, encountering bears at Yellowstone National Park can be an awe-inspiring experience, but it's essential to prioritize safety and responsible wildlife viewing. By following these safety tips and guidelines, visitors can enjoy the park's natural wonders while minimizing the risks associated with bear encounters. Remember that bears are wild animals, and our actions can impact their behavior and well-being. With proper precautions and respect for these magnificent creatures, you can create memorable and safe experiences in bear country. Yellowstone bears symbolize the park's wilderness, and protecting them ensures the preservation of this remarkable ecosystem for future generations to enjoy.

CHAPTER VII

Acadia National Park

Discovering Acadia's coastal beauty

Nestled on the rugged coastline of Maine, Acadia National Park is a gem of natural beauty and pristine wilderness. Established in 1916 as the first national park east of the Mississippi River, Acadia is a testament to the allure of coastal landscapes. Its diverse terrain, which includes granite peaks, lush forests, serene lakes, and a dramatic coastline, offers a captivating experience for visitors seeking to immerse themselves in nature's grandeur. In this section, we will embark on a journey to discover the coastal beauty of Acadia National Park, exploring its iconic features, recreational opportunities, and the enduring connection between the land and those who visit.

Acadia's most recognizable feature is undoubtedly its striking coastline. The park's shoreline is a mosaic of rocky cliffs, rugged headlands, cobblestone beaches, and picturesque inlets. One of the most iconic coastal attractions is Thunder Hole, a natural rock crevice where waves crash with tremendous force, creating a thunderous sound and impressive splashes. Visitors gather to witness this spectacle, which is most impressive during high tide.

Further along the coast, the Park Loop Road offers a scenic drive with numerous pull-offs and viewpoints, allowing travelers to take in the breathtaking vistas of the Atlantic Ocean meeting the rugged Maine coastline. Otter Cliff and Sand Beach are among the must-visit spots, providing stunning panoramas of the coast's grandeur.

Whether you're an artist seeking inspiration or a nature lover looking for tranquility, Acadia's coastline offers an abundance of visual and sensory delights.

Acadia National Park's connection to the sea extends beyond its dramatic cliffs and crashing waves. The park includes several offshore islands, including Mount Desert Island, which is the largest and the primary destination for visitors. The nearby islands of Isle au Haut, Baker Island, and Little Cranberry Island offer unique opportunities for exploration and further insights into the coastal ecosystem.

While Acadia's coastline is undoubtedly a visual masterpiece, it also provides many recreational activities. Hiking is a popular way to explore the park's coastal trails, with options ranging from easy walks to challenging cliffside scrambles. The Ocean Path, a relatively easy trail that runs parallel to the coast, offers breathtaking views and opportunities for wildlife spotting.

Rock climbing enthusiasts are drawn to the park's granite cliffs, which offer a variety of routes suitable for climbers of all levels. Precipice Trail and Jordan Cliffs Trail are well-known climbing destinations, providing both adventure and panoramic views.

For those seeking a more relaxed experience, Acadia's coastal beauty can be enjoyed from the comfort of a sea kayak or a boat tour. Guided sea kayaking excursions offer a chance to paddle along the coast, exploring hidden coves, wildlife habitats, and the fascinating interplay between land and sea. Park rangers also conduct boat tours, providing insights into the park's marine ecology and history.

The coastal beauty of Acadia National Park is not limited to its rocky shores. The park's interior harbors serene lakes and ponds that reflect the surrounding landscape like mirrors. Jordan Pond, with its crystal-clear waters and views of the Bubble Mountains, is a popular spot for leisurely strolls and enjoying afternoon tea at the Jordan Pond House.

As you delve deeper into Acadia's coastal ecosystems, you'll discover tidal pools teeming with marine life, where colorful sea anemones, crabs, and starfish thrive. These tide pools are windows into the rich diversity of coastal habitats, offering a glimpse of the intricate web of life that exists along the shoreline.

In addition to its natural beauty, Acadia National Park holds a cultural significance that adds depth to the coastal experience. Indigenous peoples, including the Wabanaki tribes, have a long history in the region, and their presence is honored through interpretive programs and exhibits within the park. The historic Jordan Pond House, dating back to the late 1800s, showcases the legacy of early settlers and serves as a reminder of the park's heritage.

The enduring connection between Acadia's coastal beauty and those who visit is a testament to the park's timeless allure. Visitors from near and far find solace, inspiration, and adventure in its coastal landscapes. Whether you're gazing out at the vast expanse of the Atlantic, exploring tide pools teeming with life, or scaling the cliffs for a bird's-eye view, Acadia National Park's coastal beauty invites you to discover the magic of the sea and the land intertwined along this enchanting stretch of the Maine coast. It is a place where the ceaseless rhythm of the tides, the sea's ever-changing colors, and the coastline's timeless grandeur converge to create an experience that leaves an indelible mark on the heart and soul.

Best hikes and scenic drives

Acadia National Park, located on the rugged coast of Maine, is a paradise for outdoor enthusiasts and nature lovers. With its dramatic coastal landscapes, lush forests, serene lakes, and pristine beaches, the park offers a wide range of hiking trails and scenic drives that showcase its coastal beauty. This section will explore some of the best hikes and scenic drives in Acadia National Park, inviting you to discover the park's remarkable coastal vistas and natural wonders.

Hiking is one of the most popular activities in Acadia National Park, and the park boasts an extensive network of well-maintained trails suitable for all skill levels. Many of these trails provide breathtaking views of the coastal beauty that defines the park.

One of the must-visit hiking destinations in Acadia is the Jordan Pond Path. This leisurely 3.3-mile loop takes you around the crystal-clear waters of Jordan Pond, offering stunning views of the iconic Bubble Mountains in the background. The trail is relatively flat, making it accessible to hikers of all ages, and it includes wooden bridges and boardwalks that enhance the experience. The Jordan Pond Path also features the Jordan Pond House, a historic establishment where you can enjoy afternoon tea or popovers with a pond view.

The Precipice Trail is a thrilling option for those seeking a more challenging hike with rewarding coastal vistas. This strenuous 1.8-mile trail leads to the summit of Champlain Mountain, offering panoramic views of the rugged coastline and the Atlantic Ocean. The trail includes sections of iron rungs and ladders, making it an exhilarating ascent. It's essential to exercise caution and wear appropriate footwear when tackling the Precipice Trail, but the views from the top are well worth the effort.

Another hiking gem in Acadia is the Ocean Path, which allows you to meander along the coast and enjoy unobstructed views of the Atlantic Ocean. This 4.4-mile trail starts at Sand Beach and leads you past iconic coastal landmarks such as Thunder Hole and Otter Cliff. The trail is relatively easy and offers numerous photography and wildlife spotting opportunities.

For those looking for a more secluded coastal hike, the Wonderland Trail is a hidden gem. This 1.4-mile loop takes you through a tranquil coastal forest, leading to tide pools along the shoreline. It's an excellent spot for exploring tidal life, including sea anemones and starfish, and offers a sense of solitude away from the park's busier trails.

In addition to hiking, Acadia National Park is known for its scenic drives that provide access to stunning coastal viewpoints and natural wonders. The Park Loop Road is a 27-mile loop that takes you on a journey through the heart of the park's coastal beauty. Along this route, you'll encounter numerous pull-offs and overlooks, allowing you to take in the breathtaking vistas of the Atlantic Ocean meeting the rugged Maine coastline.

One of the Park Loop Road highlights is Thunder Hole, where you can witness waves crashing against the rocky shore with tremendous force, creating a thunderous sound and impressive splashes. The Park Loop Road also offers access to Sand Beach, a picturesque cove with a sandy shoreline nestled between rocky cliffs. Whether you're admiring the surf or taking a dip in the ocean, Sand Beach is a perfect place to savor the coastal beauty of Acadia.

Another scenic drive that showcases the park's coastal charm is the Jordan Pond Road. This winding road takes you to the shores of Jordan Pond, where you can embark on the aforementioned Jordan Pond Path hike. The road offers glimpses of the pond's crystal-clear waters, lush forests' surrounding landscape, and the iconic Bubble Mountains.

For a more extended coastal journey, the Schoodic Peninsula is a lesser-known gem within Acadia National Park. Located on the mainland, the Schoodic Peninsula offers a quieter and less crowded experience while providing stunning coastal vistas. The Schoodic Loop Road takes you around the peninsula, passing by rocky shores, wave-splashed cliffs, and picturesque fishing villages. It's an ideal spot for picnicking, birdwatching, and enjoying the serene beauty of the Maine coast.

In conclusion, Acadia National Park's coastal beauty is a natural wonder that beckons adventurers and nature enthusiasts alike. Whether you're hiking along the park's scenic trails or embarking on a leisurely drive through its winding roads, you'll be treated to breathtaking views of the rugged coastline, pristine beaches, and serene lakes. Acadia's coastal landscapes are a testament to the power and beauty of the natural world, offering a profound connection to the ocean's timeless rhythms and the enduring allure of the Maine coast. Whether you're capturing the perfect photograph, exploring tidal pools, or simply reveling in the coastal serenity, Acadia National Park invites you to immerse yourself in the coastal beauty that defines this remarkable corner of the United States.

RV camping by the ocean

Acadia National Park, situated along the rugged coast of Maine, is a destination renowned for its coastal beauty and pristine wilderness. For outdoor enthusiasts and nature lovers who seek to immerse themselves in the splendor of the Atlantic Ocean while enjoying the comforts of an RV, the park offers a unique and captivating experience. RV camping by the ocean at Acadia National Park provides a gateway to exploration, relaxation, and the chance to create lasting memories amid one of the most picturesque coastal landscapes in the United States.

One of the primary attractions of RV camping in Acadia National Park is the opportunity to wake up to the soothing sounds of the ocean waves and the refreshing scent of saltwater in the air. Several campgrounds within the park offer RV-friendly accommodations, each with its unique charm and proximity to the ocean.

Seawall Campground, located on the western side of Mount Desert Island, is a popular choice for RV campers seeking a coastal retreat. This oceanside campground features RV sites nestled among the evergreen trees, providing a sense of privacy and tranquility. From Seawall Campground, campers can access the ocean's rocky shores, where tide pools teem with marine life, making it an ideal spot for exploration and wildlife observation.

Schoodic Woods Campground on the Schoodic Peninsula offers a serene oceanfront camping experience. This campground provides RV sites with electric hookups, modern amenities, and easy access to Schoodic Point, where dramatic cliffs meet the crashing waves of the Atlantic. The rugged coastline of the Schoodic Peninsula is a picturesque setting for coastal walks, birdwatching, and picnicking.

Blackwoods Campground, located on Mount Desert Island, is another RV-friendly option. It offers proximity to the iconic Park Loop Road and its scenic coastal vistas. RV sites at Blackwoods Campground provide a forested environment, and campers can take advantage of nearby hiking trails that lead to ocean viewpoints, such as the Ocean Path.

One of the unique aspects of RV camping at Acadia National Park is the chance to enjoy stunning ocean sunrises and sunsets from the comfort of your RV. The coastline's dramatic topography, including rocky cliffs and offshore islands, creates a breathtaking backdrop for these natural spectacles. Watching the sun dip below the horizon or witnessing the first light of day illuminate the Atlantic Ocean is a truly memorable experience that RV campers cherish.

Exploring the coastal beauty of Acadia is a fundamental part of the RV camping experience. RVers can embark on leisurely drives along the Park Loop Road, which offers numerous pull-offs and overlooks with panoramic views of the ocean meeting the rugged Maine coastline. Stops at Thunder Hole and Sand Beach are essential to take in the sights and sounds of the coastal wonders.

Hiking is another way to immerse yourself in Acadia's coastal landscapes. The Ocean Path, which runs parallel to the coast, allows RV campers to take a leisurely stroll along the shore while enjoying unobstructed views of the Atlantic. This relatively easy trail provides opportunities for photography, wildlife spotting, and serene moments by the sea.

RV campers can also venture beyond Mount Desert Island to explore the Schoodic Peninsula, where the Schoodic Loop Road provides access to pristine coastal vistas. Here, you can savor the peace and quiet of the less-traveled mainland section of Acadia while enjoying the beauty of the Maine coast.

As you camp by the ocean in Acadia National Park, you'll have the opportunity to connect with the coastal environment in unique ways. Tide pools along the shoreline are teeming with marine life, including colorful sea anemones and starfish. Exploring these tidal pools offers insights into the rich diversity of coastal ecosystems and provides a chance to witness the intricate web of life that exists along the shore.

In conclusion, RV camping by the ocean at Acadia National Park offers a blend of natural beauty, serenity, and accessibility to some of the most picturesque coastal landscapes in the United States. Whether you choose to camp at Seawall, Schoodic Woods, or Blackwoods Campground, you'll be treated to the sights and sounds of the Atlantic Ocean as it meets the rugged shores of Maine. Watching ocean sunrises and sunsets from the comfort of your RV, exploring tidal pools, and taking in the panoramic coastal views are all part of the enchanting experience of RV camping in Acadia. It's a chance to create lasting memories in a place where the ceaseless rhythm of the tides and the timeless allure of the ocean converge to create an unforgettable coastal retreat. RV campers at Acadia National Park are not only guests of nature but also participants in the ongoing story of this coastal wonderland.

Local cuisine and traditions

Acadia National Park, with its stunning coastal beauty and pristine wilderness, is a haven for outdoor enthusiasts and a place where local cuisine and traditions reflect the rich heritage of the Maine coast. While visitors come to Acadia to immerse themselves in its natural wonders, they also have the opportunity to savor the region's flavors and partake in time-honored traditions that celebrate the cultural tapestry of the area. In this section, we will explore the local cuisine and traditions that add a unique dimension to the Acadia National Park experience, inviting visitors to connect with the heritage of the Maine coast.

Lobster, often considered the quintessential seafood delicacy, plays a prominent role in the local cuisine of Acadia National Park. The Maine coast is renowned for its succulent lobsters, harvested from the cold, clear waters of the Atlantic Ocean. Visitors to the park can indulge in the classic "lobster bake" experience, where lobsters, clams, corn on the cob, and potatoes are cooked together in seaweed over an open flame. This tradition dates back to the early settlers of Maine and offers a mouthwatering taste of the sea and a connection to the region's maritime history.

Another beloved seafood dish in the Acadia region is clam chowder. Acadia's clam chowder is a comforting and hearty dish that warms the soul on chilly coastal evenings, made with tender, locally sourced clams, potatoes, onions, and a creamy broth. Pair it with freshly baked rolls or crackers for a complete coastal dining experience.

In addition to lobster and clam chowder, the Maine coast is celebrated for its delectable crab cakes, made with succulent crabmeat, breadcrumbs, and a blend of seasonings. These crab cakes, often served with a zesty aioli or a citrus-infused sauce, are a delightful appetizer or main course option for those seeking a taste of the ocean's bounty.

Acadia National Park's coastal traditions extend beyond the dining table. The art of lobstering is deeply ingrained in the local culture, and visitors can gain insights into this time-honored practice by joining lobster boat tours offered in nearby coastal towns. These tours provide an opportunity to witness lobster traps being hauled in, learn about the lifecycle of lobsters, and even participate in the process by helping to bait and set traps. It's a hands-on experience that offers a deeper appreciation for the hard work and traditions of Maine's lobster fishermen.

For those with a sweet tooth, the Maine coast is famous for its blueberry treats. Wild blueberries thrive in the acidic soils of the region, and locals have been incorporating them into various dishes for generations. Blueberry pie, blueberry pancakes, and blueberry muffins are just a few of the delightful blueberry-infused treats you can find at local bakeries and restaurants near Acadia National Park.

Traditionally, August is celebrated as the peak of the wild blueberry season, and festivals dedicated to this beloved fruit occur in nearby towns. These festivals often feature blueberry pie-eating contests, live music, craft vendors, and an abundance of blueberry-themed delicacies. Attending one of these festivals is an excellent way to immerse yourself in the local culture and enjoy the vibrant community spirit of the Maine coast.

Another coastal tradition in Acadia National Park revolves around the island communities that have thrived along the Maine coast for centuries. Many of these communities host events and festivals that showcase their unique traditions, such as boat races, traditional folk music, and craft fairs. These gatherings offer visitors a glimpse into the enduring traditions and close-knit communities that have shaped the culture of the Maine coast.

To complement the delicious cuisine and traditions of Acadia National Park, there are numerous restaurants and eateries in the nearby towns of Bar Harbor and Northeast Harbor. These establishments offer various culinary experiences, from seafood shacks serving lobster rolls to fine dining restaurants specializing in locally sourced ingredients. Dining in these coastal communities allows visitors to savor the region's flavors while enjoying the hospitality of local establishments.

In conclusion, Acadia National Park's coastal beauty is not limited to its natural landscapes; it also encompasses a rich tapestry of local cuisine and traditions. Visitors to the park can savor the flavors of the Maine coast, from lobster bakes to clam chowder and blueberry treats. They can also partake in time-honored traditions, such as lobster boat tours and blueberry festivals, that connect them to the region's cultural heritage. Whether you're indulging in a lobster dinner, joining a boat tour, or attending a coastal festival, the local cuisine and traditions of Acadia National Park add depth and flavor to the park's already captivating experience. They offer a taste of the Maine coast's history, culture, and culinary delights, making any visit to Acadia a memorable and enriching journey into the heart of coastal Maine.

CHAPTER VIII

Rocky Mountain National Park

Immersing yourself in the Rockies

Rocky Mountain National Park, located in the heart of Colorado, is a breathtaking expanse of rugged wilderness that epitomizes the grandeur of the American Rockies. Encompassing over 415 square miles of pristine alpine landscapes, this iconic national park offers visitors the opportunity to immerse themselves in the majesty of the mountains, explore pristine forests, and encounter a rich tapestry of wildlife. In this section, we will embark on a journey to discover the essence of Rocky Mountain National Park, delving into its stunning natural features, recreational activities, and the profound connection between those who visit and the untamed beauty of the Rockies.

At the core of Rocky Mountain National Park's allure are the majestic peaks and towering summits that define its skyline. The park is home to over 60 peaks that exceed 12,000 feet in elevation, including the renowned Longs Peak, which stands at 14,259 feet and beckons hikers and mountaineers worldwide. These dramatic summits are a testament to the forces of nature that shaped the region over millions of years. Exploring the park's high-altitude trails and ascending its peaks offers a unique perspective on the immensity and grandeur of the Rockies.

Among the iconic features of the park is Trail Ridge Road, the highest continuously paved road in the United States. This 48-mile scenic byway offers a breathtaking journey through the alpine tundra, with numerous overlooks providing sweeping vistas of the surrounding mountains. As visitors ascend to elevations above 12,000 feet, they are greeted with panoramic views that extend as far as the eye can see. Trail Ridge Road is a gateway to the alpine wilderness and offers a profound sense of connection to the Rockies.

Wildlife thrives in the diverse ecosystems of Rocky Mountain National Park. Elk, mule deer, bighorn sheep, and moose are among the park's charismatic megafauna. Observing these creatures in their natural habitat is a highlight for many visitors. In the fall, the park's elk populations engage in the dramatic rut, or mating season, when bugling calls and dramatic displays of dominance fill the mountain valleys.

Birdwatchers are also drawn to the park's avian diversity. From the elusive ptarmigan that blends seamlessly with the alpine tundra to the graceful American dipper that forages along mountain streams, Rocky Mountain National Park offers ample opportunities for birdwatchers to observe various species in stunning natural settings.

Hiking is one of the most popular ways to immerse oneself in the Rockies at Rocky Mountain National Park. The park boasts over 355 miles of hiking trails, ranging from easy strolls through meadows to challenging ascents of the park's towering peaks. The Bear Lake area, with its network of accessible trails, is a great place to start for hikers of all levels. Trails like the Emerald Lake Trail and the Alberta Falls Trail offer a glimpse of the park's stunning alpine landscapes.

For more adventurous hikers, Longs Peak presents the ultimate challenge. The Keyhole Route, a demanding 14-mile round-trip ascent, takes climbers to the summit of this iconic peak. Along the way, hikers encounter a variety of alpine environments, including the Boulder Field and the Narrows. The sense of accomplishment upon reaching the summit and gazing out across the vast expanse of the Rockies is unparalleled.

Fishing is another popular activity in the park, with numerous pristine mountain lakes and streams teeming with trout. Anglers can cast their lines into crystal-clear waters while surrounded by breathtaking scenery. Whether fly fishing along the Big Thompson River or seeking solitude at an alpine lake, the park's waters offer both relaxation and a connection to the natural world.

Rocky Mountain National Park also provides opportunities for experiencing the Rockies on horseback. Guided horseback rides take visitors through alpine meadows, dense forests, and pristine valleys, offering a unique perspective on the park's natural beauty. Riding through the park's diverse terrain under the watchful gaze of towering peaks is a memorable way to immerse oneself in the Rockies.

Camping is a popular way to connect with the wilderness at Rocky Mountain National Park. The park offers a range of camping options, from developed campgrounds with modern amenities to backcountry campsites for those seeking a more remote experience. Camping in the Rockies allows visitors to witness star-filled night skies, listen to the calls of nocturnal wildlife, and wake up to the crisp mountain air.

In addition to its stunning natural features and recreational activities, Rocky Mountain National Park is also a place where visitors can forge a profound connection to the Rockies. The park's preservation and conservation efforts ensure that future generations can continue to immerse themselves in its pristine landscapes and experience the enduring beauty of the American Rockies.

In conclusion, Rocky Mountain National Park is a sanctuary of untamed beauty and an opportunity for visitors to immerse themselves in the majesty of the Rockies. The park offers many ways to connect with the natural world, from its towering peaks and alpine meadows to its diverse wildlife and outdoor activities. Whether you're hiking to a mountain summit, observing wildlife in its habitat, or simply taking in the breathtaking views along Trail Ridge Road, Rocky Mountain National Park invites you to embrace the essence of the Rockies and discover the timeless allure of this extraordinary wilderness. It is a place where the mountains stand as sentinels of nature's grandeur, and the rugged beauty of the Rockies forever leaves its mark on the hearts and souls of those who venture into its embrace.

Hiking through alpine landscapes

Rocky Mountain National Park, situated in the heart of Colorado, is a hiker's paradise, offering an unparalleled opportunity to explore the stunning alpine landscapes of the American Rockies. With over 355 miles of hiking trails, the park allows hikers of all levels to immerse themselves in pristine wilderness, experience breathtaking vistas, and connect with the natural world. In this section, we will embark on a journey through the alpine landscapes of Rocky Mountain National Park, exploring the diverse trails, the unique ecosystems, and the sense of wonder that comes with each step taken in this magnificent wilderness.

One of the defining features of hiking in Rocky Mountain National Park is the chance to traverse diverse ecosystems as you ascend through elevation zones. The park's trails take you through montane forests, subalpine meadows, and into the high-alpine tundra. Each elevation zone reveals its unique beauty and offers a glimpse into the adaptations of the plants and wildlife that call these landscapes home.

Starting from the lower elevations, the park's montane forests are lush with coniferous trees, including ponderosa pine, Douglas fir, and lodgepole pine. Hiking through these forests is a serene experience, with sunlight filtering through the towering trees and the soothing sound of birdsong filling the air. Trails like the Cub Lake Trail and the Gem Lake Trail lead hikers through these enchanting woods, with opportunities to spot wildlife such as mule deer and songbirds.

As you gain elevation, subalpine meadows offer expansive vistas of wildflowers, clear streams, and abundant wildlife. The Bear Lake area is a prime location for experiencing these subalpine landscapes, with trails like the Flattop Mountain Trail and the Dream Lake Trail leading through subalpine meadows filled with colorful blooms during the summer months. It's a place where the views of surrounding peaks and the chance to spot marmots, elk, and ptarmigan add to the sense of wonder.

Continuing upward, the high-alpine tundra awaits those who venture into the park's higher elevations. Here, the landscape is marked by rugged rocks, alpine lakes, and hardy vegetation adapted to the harsh alpine environment. The alpine tundra is a fragile ecosystem where plant life, including alpine avens and cushion plants, have evolved to withstand extreme temperatures and high winds. Hiking to places like Chasm Lake or Andrews Glacier allows hikers to experience the unique beauty and solitude of the high-alpine terrain, where the views stretch as far as the eye can see.

Among the most iconic hikes in Rocky Mountain National Park is the ascent of Longs Peak, the park's tallest mountain. The Keyhole Route, a challenging 14-mile round-trip hike, takes adventurers through all three elevation zones, from the montane forests to the alpine tundra. As hikers ascend the Keyhole, a dramatic rock formation that marks the route's transition to the tundra, they are rewarded with panoramic views that reveal the true scale of the Rockies. The sense of accomplishment upon reaching the summit and looking out across the vast expanse of the park is unparalleled.

For those seeking a less strenuous but equally rewarding alpine experience, the Trail Ridge Road offers a high-altitude journey by car or shuttle bus. This 48-mile scenic byway takes travelers through the alpine tundra and provides numerous overlooks that offer sweeping vistas of the surrounding mountains. It's an opportunity to embrace the grandeur of the Rockies without the need for a demanding hike, making it accessible to visitors of all ages and abilities.

While hiking through Rocky Mountain National Park's alpine landscapes, encounters with wildlife are a common and cherished experience. Elk, mule deer, and bighorn sheep are often spotted along the park's trails, and observant hikers may encounter smaller mammals such as pikas and marmots. The park's high-altitude meadows are also prime habitat for birdwatchers, with species like the white-tailed ptarmigan and American pipit making their homes in the alpine tundra.

For those interested in alpine wildflowers, the park offers a colorful spectacle during the summer months. Subalpine and alpine meadows burst with blooms, with species such as columbines, Indian paintbrush, and alpine sunflowers creating a vibrant tapestry of colors. Photographers and nature enthusiasts are drawn to these areas, where the delicate beauty of wildflowers is juxtaposed against the rugged backdrop of the Rockies.
In conclusion, hiking through the alpine landscapes of Rocky Mountain National Park is a journey of discovery and wonder. The park's diverse elevation zones, from montane forests to high-alpine tundra, offer a rich tapestry of natural beauty and a profound connection to the natural world. Whether you're ascending Longs Peak,

exploring subalpine meadows, or gazing out from a Trail Ridge Road overlook, each step taken in this magnificent wilderness reveals a new facet of the Rockies' grandeur. Rocky Mountain National Park invites hikers to embrace the essence of the American Rockies, witness the resilience of alpine ecosystems, and create lasting memories amid some of the most breathtaking landscapes that nature has to offer. It's a place where the mountains stand as sentinels of untamed beauty, and the call of the alpine tundra beckons those who seek to immerse themselves in the majesty of the Rockies.

RV campgrounds with mountain views

Rocky Mountain National Park, nestled in the heart of Colorado, is a place where the majesty of the Rockies unfolds before your eyes. For those seeking an immersive experience in this pristine wilderness, RV camping provides a perfect blend of comfort and access to the park's natural beauty. What sets RV camping in Rocky Mountain National Park apart is the opportunity to wake up to breathtaking mountain views, dine beneath star-studded skies, and connect with the alpine wilderness like never before. This section will explore the RV campgrounds within the park that offer stunning mountain vistas, ensuring an unforgettable Rocky Mountain experience.

Aspenglen Campground, located on the park's eastern side, is a picturesque RV campground that offers mountain views and easy access to some of the park's most iconic trails. Nestled among a forest of tall pine trees, Aspenglen provides a serene and shaded setting for RV campers. The campground's proximity to the Fall River Entrance makes it an ideal starting point for exploring the park's eastern side. From here, you can embark on hikes to destinations such as Alberta Falls and The Pool, where you'll encounter pristine mountain streams and cascading waterfalls.

Further into the park, Moraine Park Campground is another RV-friendly destination that boasts stunning mountain views. Set in a wide valley surrounded by towering peaks, Moraine Park offers a sense of grandeur that's hard to match. The campground provides both electric and non-electric RV sites, accommodating a variety of camping preferences. You can take a short drive from Moraine Park to the iconic Bear Lake area, where many hiking trails lead to alpine lakes and panoramic viewpoints. It's also a prime location for wildlife viewing, with elk frequently grazing in the meadows.

For RV campers seeking a more remote and rustic experience, Timber Creek Campground is the westernmost campground in the park and offers breathtaking mountain views of the Never Summer Mountains. This campground is excellent for those who appreciate a quieter atmosphere and a closer connection to the wilderness. From Timber Creek, you can explore the park's western side, which features pristine alpine lakes, old-growth forests, and opportunities for birdwatching and stargazing. The nearby Colorado River Trail is a favorite among hikers, providing access to the park's high country and stunning mountain vistas. Perhaps one of the most coveted RV campgrounds in Rocky Mountain National Park is the Moraine Park Campground. Located in a picturesque valley surrounded by towering peaks, Moraine Park offers a sense of grandeur that's hard to match. The campground provides both electric and non-electric RV sites, accommodating a variety of camping preferences. You can take a short drive from Moraine Park to the iconic Bear Lake area, where many hiking trails lead to alpine lakes and panoramic viewpoints. It's also a prime location for wildlife viewing, with elk frequently grazing in the meadows.

One of the unique aspects of RV camping at Moraine Park Campground is the opportunity to witness the elk rut, a dramatic and often noisy event that occurs in the fall. As the male elk, or bulls, vie for the attention of females, or cows, their bugling calls echo through the valley, creating a truly immersive wildlife experience. For RV campers looking to connect with the rhythms of nature and witness this awe-inspiring spectacle, Moraine Park is the place to be.

The Longs Peak Campground is an excellent choice for a more secluded RV camping experience with mountain views. Located at a higher elevation, this campground offers cooler temperatures and proximity to the park's iconic Longs Peak, which stands at 14,259 feet. The campground provides RV sites with electric hookups and offers a serene setting among ponderosa pine and aspen trees. From Longs Peak Campground, you can explore the surrounding area, including the Longs Peak Trailhead, which is the starting point for those attempting to summit this iconic mountain.

In addition to these campgrounds, Rocky Mountain National Park offers several others, each with its unique charm and access to mountain views. Whether you choose to camp at Aspenglen, Moraine Park, Timber Creek, or Longs Peak, you'll have the opportunity to wake up to the sight of towering peaks, dine beneath star-studded skies, and immerse yourself in the unparalleled beauty of the Rockies.

It's important to note that Rocky Mountain National Park RV campgrounds can fill up quickly, especially during the peak summer months. Reservations are highly recommended, and campers should plan ahead to secure their spot. Additionally, campers should be aware of park regulations and practice Leave No Trace principles to ensure the preservation of this pristine wilderness.

In conclusion, RV campgrounds with mountain views at Rocky Mountain National Park offer a unique and immersive experience in one of America's most stunning natural landscapes. Whether you choose to camp at Aspenglen, Moraine Park, Timber Creek, or Longs Peak, you'll be treated to breathtaking vistas of the Rockies, access to iconic hiking trails, and the chance to connect with the wilderness. RV camping in Rocky Mountain National Park is not just a vacation; it's an opportunity to wake up in the heart of the Rockies and experience the majestic beauty of this remarkable national park. It's a chance to create lasting memories amid the splendor of the mountains, where every day begins and ends with awe-inspiring views of the Rockies' towering peaks.

Wildlife photography opportunities

Rocky Mountain National Park, located in the heart of Colorado, is a sanctuary for wildlife enthusiasts and photographers alike. With its diverse ecosystems, including montane forests, subalpine meadows, and high- alpine tundra, the park offers a rich tapestry of habitats home to various animal species. From iconic megafauna like elk and bighorn sheep to elusive predators like coyotes and bobcats, the park provides countless opportunities for wildlife photographers to capture Rocky Mountain wildlife's natural beauty and behavior. In this section, we will explore the unique wildlife photography opportunities that await in this remarkable national park.

The majestic elk is one of the most sought-after subjects for wildlife photographers at Rocky Mountain National Park. These iconic creatures are abundant in the park, providing numerous opportunities for photographers to capture their striking presence. During the fall rutting season, male elk, or bulls, engage in dramatic displays of dominance and compete for the attention of females, or cows. The bugling calls of the bulls echo through the valleys, creating an unforgettable and photogenic spectacle. Photographers often visit areas like Moraine Park and Horseshoe Park, where elk congregate during the rut to capture these moments. The combination of dramatic behavior and the park's stunning landscapes makes for compelling wildlife photography.

Bighorn sheep are another charismatic species that are frequently photographed in Rocky Mountain National Park. These agile climbers are well adapted to the park's rugged terrain and can often be spotted perched on steep cliffs and rocky outcrops. During the rutting season, male bighorn sheep, or rams, engage in head-to-head battles for dominance, providing photographers with opportunities to capture their powerful and dynamic interactions. Areas like Sheep Lakes and the aptly named Bighorn Sheep Canyon are reliable locations for photographing these impressive animals against the backdrop of the Rockies.

For birdwatchers and bird photographers, Rocky Mountain National Park offers a diverse array of avian species in stunning natural settings. The park's subalpine and alpine meadows are prime habitat for various birdlife, including the white-tailed ptarmigan, which is specially adapted to life in the high-altitude tundra. These camouflaged birds blend seamlessly with their alpine surroundings, making them a challenging yet rewarding subject for wildlife photographers. Patient observers may also spot other alpine species like the American pipit and the Clark's nutcracker, which thrive in the harsh conditions of the park's high country.

The park's montane forests provide habitat for numerous bird species, including the vibrant and melodious American robin, mountain bluebird, and Steller's jay. These forests are alive with bird activity, and photographers can capture intimate moments such as feeding, courtship displays, and nest-building. The diversity of birdlife in the park ensures that there's always something fascinating to observe and photograph.

In addition to larger mammals and birds, Rocky Mountain National Park is home to smaller but equally captivating creatures. Pikas, often called "rock rabbits," are found in the park's high-alpine environments. These tiny, round mammals are known for their high-pitched calls and their habit of collecting and storing food for the winter. Photographing pikas in their rocky habitats can be a delightful challenge for wildlife enthusiasts, as their small size and rapid movements make them elusive subjects.

Coyotes are another intriguing subject for wildlife photographers in the park. These adaptable predators are often seen in the park's open meadows and grasslands, where they hunt for small mammals and birds. Their behavior, from hunting to playful interactions, provides photographers with many opportunities to capture their elusive nature. Patient observation and a telephoto lens can yield stunning images of coyotes against the backdrop of the Rockies.

For those who are truly fortunate, encounters with more elusive predators like bobcats and mountain lions can result in remarkable wildlife photography. These solitary and elusive animals are rarely seen, but their presence in the park adds to its wild and untamed character. Photographers who can capture images of these elusive creatures in their natural habitat often produce exceptional and highly sought-after wildlife photography. When photographing Rocky Mountain National Park wildlife, it's essential to prioritize safety and ethical behavior. Park regulations require visitors to maintain a safe distance from animals and to avoid disturbing their natural behaviors. This ensures the well-being of the wildlife and allows photographers to capture more authentic and compelling images. Patience, respect for the animals, and knowledge of their behavior are key to successful wildlife photography in the park.

In conclusion, Rocky Mountain National Park is a paradise for wildlife photographers, offering many opportunities to capture the natural beauty and behavior of the park's diverse animal species. The park's ecosystems provide a rich tapestry of subjects and settings, from the dramatic elk rut to the agile bighorn sheep, the vibrant birdlife to the elusive predators. Photographers who venture into this wilderness are rewarded with breathtaking images that capture the essence of the Rockies and the untamed beauty of Rocky Mountain wildlife. It's a place where every click of the camera shutter tells a story of the natural world, where the majesty of the Rockies is reflected in the eyes of its inhabitants, and where the art of wildlife photography comes to life in the heart of Colorado's wilderness.

CHAPTER IX

Wrangell-St. Elias National Park

Remote adventures in Alaska

Nestled in the vast wilderness of Alaska, Wrangell-St. Elias National Park and Preserve is a testament to the untamed beauty of America's largest national park. Covering over 13 million acres, it dwarfs even the grandest of landscapes, and its remoteness offers a unique opportunity for adventurers seeking the ultimate escape into the wild. This park, with its rugged mountains, sprawling glaciers, and pristine rivers, invites those with a spirit of exploration to embark on remote adventures that unveil the true essence of Alaska's wilderness. This section will delve into the remote adventures that await intrepid travelers in Wrangell-St. Elias National Park explores the majestic landscapes, thrilling activities, and the sense of isolation that defines this extraordinary destination.

One of the defining features of Wrangell-St. Elias National Park is its vast and rugged terrain, dominated by the towering peaks of the Wrangell and St. Elias mountain ranges. These mountains, some of the highest in North America, create a dramatic and awe-inspiring backdrop for adventurers. The park is home to nine of the 16 highest peaks in the United States, including Mount St. Elias, which soars to over 18,000 feet. The ruggedness of these mountains is a challenge that beckons climbers and mountaineers worldwide, offering the opportunity to conquer peaks that few have summited.

Mountaineering in Wrangell-St. Elias National Park is not for the faint of heart. The remote and unpredictable nature of the terrain, combined with Alaska's unpredictable weather, makes it a true test of skill and endurance. Climbers must be self-reliant and well-prepared for the challenges that await them. However, the rewards are immeasurable, with the chance to stand on the summits of towering peaks and gaze out across the vast wilderness below.

Glaciers are a defining feature of the park's landscape, covering nearly a quarter of its total area. These massive rivers of ice are a testament to the power of nature, and they provide unique opportunities for exploration. Adventurers can embark on glacier hikes, traverse icy landscapes, and even explore ice caves hidden beneath the glacier's surface. The Root Glacier, located in the park's Kennecott Valley, is a popular destination for glacier treks, offering a surreal and otherworldly experience as you navigate the icy expanse.

In addition to mountaineering and glacier exploration, Wrangell-St. Elias National Park offers thrilling opportunities for backcountry backpacking and camping. The park's remote wilderness allows backpackers to experience true solitude and self-reliance. Trails are minimal, and often the only routes are those created by wildlife. For those willing to embrace the challenge, this is a chance to immerse oneself in the wild, far from the sights and sounds of civilization.

Backcountry camping in Wrangell-St. Elias National Park allows adventurers to witness the breathtaking beauty of the Alaskan wilderness up close. You can set up camp beneath the towering peaks, beside pristine rivers, or in lush alpine meadows. The experience is one of complete immersion in nature, where the only company may be the calls of birds and the occasional sighting of wildlife.

Wildlife enthusiasts will find Wrangell-St. Elias National Park is a haven for observing and photographing various species. The park has various animals, including moose, Dall sheep, caribou, grizzly bears, and wolves. The remote and rugged terrain provides ample opportunities for wildlife sightings, and those with patience and a keen eye can capture the natural behaviors of these creatures in their unspoiled habitats.

One of the most iconic adventures in the park is rafting and kayaking along its pristine rivers. The park's braided glacial rivers, like the Copper and Chitina Rivers, offer exhilarating journeys through some of Alaska's most remote and untouched landscapes. Rafters can navigate through canyons, float past glaciers, and camp on remote riverbanks. The feeling of isolation and connection to nature is palpable as you glide down these wild rivers, surrounded by the towering peaks of the Wrangell and St. Elias ranges.

To truly appreciate the remoteness of Wrangell-St. Elias National Park, one must venture to the historic Kennecott Mines, a designated National Historic Landmark within the park. The Kennecott Mines, once a thriving copper mining operation, now stands as a relic of the past and a testament to human perseverance in the wilderness. Visitors can explore the abandoned buildings and structures, offering a glimpse into the challenges faced by those who sought their fortune in this rugged land.

The isolation of Wrangell-St. Elias National Park is a double-edged sword. While it offers unparalleled opportunities for remote adventures, it also presents challenges in terms of access and logistics. The park's vastness and rugged terrain mean that reaching many areas requires careful planning, whether by small aircraft, bush plane, or hiking through the wilderness. Visitors must be prepared for the remote nature of the park, with limited services and amenities available.

In conclusion, Wrangell-St. Elias National Park is a place of unparalleled remote adventures, where intrepid travelers can immerse themselves in the wild beauty of Alaska's wilderness. The park's towering mountains, sprawling glaciers, pristine rivers, and diverse wildlife offer a wealth of experiences for those who seek to explore its vast and rugged terrain. Whether it's mountaineering on towering peaks, hiking through the backcountry, rafting down wild rivers, or simply witnessing the park's breathtaking landscapes, Wrangell- St. Elias National Park invites adventurers to embrace the true essence of remote Alaska. It's a place where the spirit of exploration thrives, the wilderness stretches as far as the eye can see, and where the call of the wild is answered by those seeking to venture into its heart.

Backcountry exploration and camping

Wrangell-St. Elias National Park and Preserve, situated in the rugged wilderness of Alaska, is a vast and untamed expanse that beckons adventurers seeking a truly immersive backcountry experience. Covering over 13 million acres, it is not only America's largest national park but also a place where the call of the wild is answered by those who yearn for remote exploration. Within this pristine wilderness, backcountry exploration and camping offer a unique opportunity to delve deep into the heart of Alaska's wild landscapes, far from the trappings of modern civilization. This section will journey into the backcountry exploration and camping world at Wrangell- St. Elias National Park explores this remote adventure's challenges, rewards, and profound connection to nature.

At the core of backcountry exploration in Wrangell-St. Elias is the desire to escape the beaten path and venture into the unknown. The park's rugged and remote terrain often leaves travelers with minimal trails and human-made routes. Instead, the paths are shaped by wildlife, time, and the forces of nature. This means that backcountry adventurers must be self-reliant, prepared, and adaptable. Navigating this untamed wilderness may involve route-finding skills, river crossings, and a deep appreciation for solitude.

One of the critical elements of backcountry exploration in Wrangell-St. Elias is backpacking, where travelers carry all they need for survival on their backs. The park's extensive trail system, while minimal compared to other national parks, provides access to some of Alaska's most remote and beautiful landscapes. Hiking through the backcountry allows adventurers to immerse themselves in pristine forests, traverse open meadows, and ascend to high-alpine environments, all while witnessing breathtaking views of the park's rugged mountains and glaciers.

Backcountry camping in Wrangell-St. Elias National Park is a chance to connect with the wilderness profoundly. Unlike camping in established campgrounds, where amenities and services are readily available, backcountry campers must be entirely self-sufficient. This means carrying the basics for survival—food, shelter, and clothing—and adhering to Leave No Trace principles to minimize their environmental impact. Campers must also be vigilant in bear country, employing bear-proof food storage methods and maintaining a safe distance from wildlife.

The park offers numerous backcountry camping opportunities, with designated campsites spread throughout its vast expanse. These campsites are strategically located to provide access to key attractions and allow travelers to explore different aspects of the park's diverse ecosystems. Whether you camp beside a pristine river, beneath towering peaks, or in a lush alpine meadow, the experience is a complete immersion in nature. The only sounds may be the calls of birds and the rustling of leaves in the wind.

For those who crave the ultimate backcountry adventure, multi-day backpacking trips provide the opportunity to journey deep into the park's wilderness. Routes like the Nizina River Corridor and the Skolai Pass offer extended treks through some of the most remote and stunning landscapes. These journeys require careful planning, including mapping out routes, understanding river crossings, and assessing the availability of water sources. While challenging, they offer an unparalleled sense of freedom and self-sufficiency.

The remote nature of Wrangell-St. Elias National Park also means that travelers are treated to some of the darkest skies in the United States. Far from the light pollution of urban areas, backcountry campers can witness a celestial display that is nothing short of awe-inspiring. The stars, planets, and the Milky Way become vividly visible, creating a connection to the cosmos that is increasingly rare in our modern world.

Backcountry exploration and camping at Wrangell-St. Elias National Park are not without their challenges. The park's remote and unpredictable weather, with sudden storms and rapidly changing conditions, requires careful preparation and resilience. Travelers must also be prepared for encounters with wildlife, including grizzly bears and other large mammals. Carrying bear-resistant food containers and practicing proper bear safety measures is essential for a safe and responsible wilderness experience.

Despite these challenges, the rewards of backcountry exploration and camping in Wrangell-St. Elias are immeasurable. The sense of isolation and connection to nature are profound, allowing travelers to disconnect from the distractions of daily life and immerse themselves in the beauty of the Alaskan wilderness. It's a place where the spirit of exploration thrives, where every step taken into the backcountry reveals a new facet of the natural world, and where the majesty of the park's towering peaks and sprawling glaciers leaves an indelible mark on the soul.

In conclusion, backcountry exploration and camping at Wrangell-St. Elias National Park offer intrepid travelers a chance to journey deep into the heart of Alaska's wilderness. The rugged terrain, minimal trails, and self-reliance required for this adventure create a profound and transformative connection to nature. Whether backpacking through pristine forests, traversing open meadows, or ascending to high-alpine environments, every moment spent in the backcountry is a step into the unknown. Wrangell-St. Elias National Park beckons those who seek to answer the call of the wild and venture into its remote and untamed landscapes, where the essence of Alaska's wilderness is revealed in all its raw and untouched beauty.

Navigating the challenges of Alaska's wilderness

Wrangell-St. Elias National Park and Preserve, located in the rugged wilderness of Alaska, is a land of extremes and untamed beauty. Covering an astonishing 13 million acres, it stands as America's largest national park, offering a unique blend of grandeur and wilderness. Yet, with its remoteness, harsh climate, and vast, rugged terrain, navigating the challenges of this park requires careful planning, resilience, and a deep respect for the forces of nature. This section will explore the many challenges adventurers face in Alaska's wilderness at Wrangell-St. Elias National Park and the skills and mindset required to overcome them.

One of the first challenges that visitors to Wrangell-St. Elias National Park encounter is its sheer size and remoteness. The park's vastness is on a scale that can be difficult to comprehend, and reaching its interior often requires long journeys through the Alaskan wilderness. Roads are limited, and many areas are only accessible by small aircraft, bush plane, or by hiking and backpacking. This means that travelers must be prepared for extended periods of isolation and self-sufficiency and have a heightened awareness of the logistics involved in reaching and exploring the park's remote locations.

Alaska's unpredictable weather is another significant challenge for those venturing into Wrangell-St. Elias National Park. The park experiences a continental climate, with cold winters and variable weather patterns. Sudden storms, heavy snowfall, and rapidly changing conditions are common, even during summer. Travelers must be prepared for the full spectrum of weather, from sweltering heat to bitter cold, and from clear skies to whiteout blizzards. Adequate clothing, shelter, and equipment are essential to ensure safety and comfort in this challenging climate.

Navigating the park's rugged terrain is a test of both physical and mental endurance. The Wrangell and St. Elias mountain ranges create a dramatic and unforgiving landscape with their towering peaks and sprawling glaciers. Hiking and backpacking often involve negotiating steep slopes, crossing swift glacial rivers, and navigating through dense forests. This challenging terrain demands a high level of fitness and outdoor skills. Hikers and backpackers should be prepared for route-finding, river crossings, and steep ascents and descents while carrying essential gear and supplies on their backs.

River crossings, in particular, are a noteworthy challenge in the park's backcountry. Alaska's glacial rivers are swift, cold, and often unbridged. Travelers must use caution and proper techniques to navigate these crossings safely. Techniques such as fording, using trekking poles for stability, and assessing water depth and current speed are crucial for a successful river crossing. Additionally, travelers should be aware of changing water levels due to weather conditions or glacial melt, which can significantly impact river crossings.

The park's isolation means that visitors must be entirely self-sufficient. Limited services and amenities are available within the park, and travelers must come prepared with all the necessary supplies, including food, water, clothing, and camping gear. Backcountry camping is common in the park, and campers must adhere to Leave No Trace principles to minimize their environmental impact. Proper food storage, particularly in bear country, is crucial to ensure both safety and wildlife protection.

Wildlife encounters are another challenge in Wrangell-St. Elias National Park is where grizzly bears and other large mammals roam freely. Travelers must be well-versed in bear safety protocols, including carrying bear-resistant food containers and practicing safe storage and disposal of food and trash. Maintaining a safe distance from wildlife is essential for both the well-being of visitors and the protection of the park's inhabitants.

For those seeking the ultimate adventure, mountaineering in Wrangell-St. Elias National Park presents an array of challenges and rewards. The park's high peaks, frigid temperatures, and unpredictable weather make mountaineering here a test of skill and endurance. Climbers must be self-reliant and well-prepared, carrying specialized gear and equipment to navigate crevassed glaciers, steep rock faces, and extreme altitudes. The remote nature of these peaks means that rescue and assistance are often far from reach, requiring climbers to be entirely self-sufficient.

Despite these challenges, the rewards of conquering Wrangell-St. Elias National Park's peaks are immeasurable. Standing atop these towering summits, with sweeping vistas of the park's vast wilderness, offers an unparalleled sense of accomplishment and connection to the natural world. It is a reminder of the indomitable spirit of adventure and the enduring allure of untamed landscapes.

In conclusion, navigating the challenges of Alaska's wilderness at Wrangell-St. Elias National Park is a test of physical stamina, outdoor skills, and mental fortitude. The park's remoteness, unpredictable weather, rugged terrain, river crossings, and wildlife encounters demand careful planning, preparation, and a deep respect for the natural world. Yet, it is precisely these challenges that make the park a haven for those who seek the ultimate adventure and an opportunity to immerse themselves in the pristine beauty of the Alaskan wilderness. It's a place where travelers are invited to push their boundaries, embrace the unknown, and forge a profound connection to the untamed grandeur of Wrangell-St. Elias National Park.

Unique experiences in the park

Wrangell-St. Elias National Park and Preserve, located in the remote wilderness of Alaska, offers a wealth of unique experiences that set it apart as one of the most extraordinary destinations in the United States. Encompassing over 13 million acres of pristine wilderness, it is not only America's largest national park but also a place where visitors can immerse themselves in Alaska's raw beauty and untamed landscapes. In this section, we will explore some of the remarkable and distinctive experiences that await those who venture into this vast and rugged park, from glacier hiking and flightseeing to cultural exploration and the thrill of remote adventures.

One of the most iconic and unique experiences at Wrangell-St. Elias National Park is exploring its sprawling glaciers. With a significant portion of the park covered by glaciers, visitors can embark on glacier hikes that take them into a world of ice and awe-inspiring beauty. The Root Glacier, located in the park's Kennecott Valley, is a popular destination for glacier treks. Adventurers can don crampons and explore the glacier's otherworldly terrain, navigating through ice caves, icefalls, and crevasses. The sensation of walking on ice, surrounded by towering ice walls and the sounds of trickling meltwater, creates an unforgettable and surreal experience.

Flightseeing is another unique way to appreciate the grandeur of Wrangell-St. Elias National Park. The park's vastness and remote terrain make it challenging to explore entirely by land, but from the air, visitors can gain a perspective that reveals the full extent of its rugged beauty. Numerous air tour operators offer flights that provide breathtaking aerial views of the park's towering mountain ranges, glaciers, and vast expanses of wilderness. Flightseeing not only allows visitors to grasp the park's scale but also offers a chance to spot wildlife from above, including bears, moose, and Dall sheep.

The park's rich cultural history and the remnants of the Kennecott Mines create a unique opportunity for historical exploration. Wrangell-St. Elias National Park is home to the Kennecott Mines National Historic Landmark, a preserved copper mining complex that offers a glimpse into Alaska's industrial past. Visitors can tour the well-preserved buildings, including the 14-story Kennecott Concentration Mill, and learn about the challenges and triumphs of the people who once lived and worked in this remote area. The combination of natural beauty and historical intrigue makes the Kennecott Mines a distinctive attraction within the park.

For those seeking remote adventures and the ultimate escape into the wild, Wrangell-St. Elias National Park delivers unparalleled opportunities. The park's vast wilderness and rugged terrain invite intrepid travelers to explore its backcountry, where minimal trails and minimal human presence create a sense of isolation and self-sufficiency. Multi-day backpacking trips through the park's wilderness offer a chance to disconnect from the modern world and immerse oneself in the raw beauty of Alaska's wilderness. Travelers must be well-prepared, as the challenges of navigating the remote backcountry are significant, but the rewards are immeasurable.

Wildlife enthusiasts will find Wrangell-St. Elias National Park to be a haven for observing and photographing a variety of species. The park's diverse ecosystems, from dense forests to alpine tundra, provide habitat for numerous animals, including moose, Dall sheep, caribou, grizzly bears, and wolves. The remote and untouched nature of the park ensures that wildlife sightings are frequent and often up close. Patient observers may capture the natural behaviors of these creatures in their pristine habitats, creating memorable and authentic wildlife encounters.

Exploring the park's historic mining sites offers a glimpse into the challenges and triumphs of those who once lived and worked in this remote area. The Kennecott Mines National Historic Landmark is the centerpiece of historical exploration in the park, with well-preserved buildings and exhibits that tell the story of Alaska's copper mining industry. Visitors can step back in time as they tour the mining complex, walk the wooden boardwalks of the historic townsite, and learn about the lives of the miners and their families.

Dark skies and celestial wonders await stargazers in Wrangell-St. Elias National Park. The park's remote location, far from the light pollution of urban areas, provides an ideal environment for stargazing and astrophotography. On clear nights, visitors can witness a breathtaking display of stars, planets, and the Milky Way. The celestial panorama is a reminder of the vastness of the universe and a chance to connect with the cosmos in an increasingly rare way in our modern world.

In conclusion, Wrangell-St. Elias National Park offers a tapestry of unique and unforgettable experiences that set it apart as one of the most remarkable destinations in the United States. From glacier hiking and flightseeing to historical exploration of the Kennecott Mines, from remote adventures in the backcountry to wildlife encounters and stargazing, the park invites visitors to immerse themselves in the untamed beauty of Alaska's wilderness. It is a place where the spirit of adventure thrives, where every day brings new discoveries, and where the essence of the park's grandeur leaves an indelible mark on the soul. Wrangell-St. Elias National Park is an invitation to explore, discover, and be forever transformed by its unique experiences.

CONCLUSION

In conclusion, "Scenic Stays: The RV Camper's Journey Through National Parks" is a captivating and informative guide that celebrates the beauty, adventure, and serenity of exploring our nation's remarkable national parks from the comfort of an RV. Throughout the pages of this book, we have embarked on a thrilling odyssey through some of the most iconic and awe-inspiring landscapes that North America has to offer.

Our journey began with exploring the RV lifestyle, delving into the intricacies of selecting the right RV, equipping it for the road, and ensuring its safety and maintenance. Armed with knowledge and preparedness, we then embarked on the exciting task of selecting the national parks that would become our destinations. With over 60 national parks to choose from, we considered factors like geography, climate, and the unique features of each park to curate a list of must-visit destinations.

The book then guided us through the essential steps of planning our adventure, from booking campsites and securing permits to creating a well-organized travel itinerary that ensures we make the most of our time in each park. We explored the significance of responsible waste management, conservation, and eco-friendly practices during our RV journey, understanding that our actions can have a lasting impact on these pristine natural habitats.

As we ventured into the heart of each national park, the book provided us with invaluable insights into the park's history, geology, flora, and fauna. We discovered the best hiking trails, scenic overlooks, and hidden gems, allowing us to connect deeply with the natural wonders surrounding us. We also celebrated the diverse array of outdoor activities available, from kayaking and wildlife viewing to stargazing beneath the vast night sky.

Throughout our journey, "Scenic Stays" emphasized the importance of mindfulness, respect for nature, and leaving no trace. We were reminded that while we seek to immerse ourselves in the beauty of these national parks, we also bear the responsibility of preserving and protecting them for future generations to enjoy.

In the end, "Scenic Stays: The RV Camper's Journey Through National Parks" is not just a guidebook; it is an invitation to embark on a life-changing adventure. It encourages us to embrace the freedom and flexibility of the RV lifestyle, to disconnect from the hustle and bustle of daily life, and to reconnect with the natural world in all its splendor.

This book is a tribute to the breathtaking landscapes, the diverse ecosystems, and the rich cultural heritage that make our national parks so extraordinary. It inspires us to become stewards of the environment, to appreciate the simple joys of life on the road, and to forge lasting memories with loved ones against the backdrop of some of the most awe-inspiring scenery on Earth.

So, as you prepare to embark on your own RV journey through national parks, may this book be your trusted companion and source of inspiration. May it remind you that adventure awaits just beyond the horizon, that the beauty of our world is boundless, and that the open road is your gateway to discovery. Safe travels, fellow adventurers, and may your scenic stays in our national parks be filled with wonder, reverence, and unforgettable moments that will last a lifetime.

Thank you for buying and reading/listening to our book. If you found this book useful/helpful please take a few minutes and leave a review on the platform where you purchased our book. Your feedback matters greatly to us.